This Book

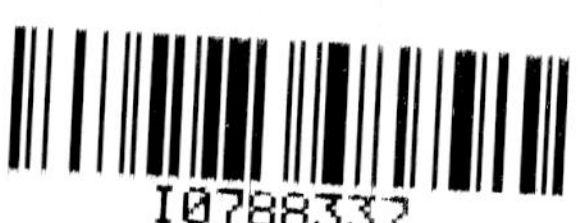

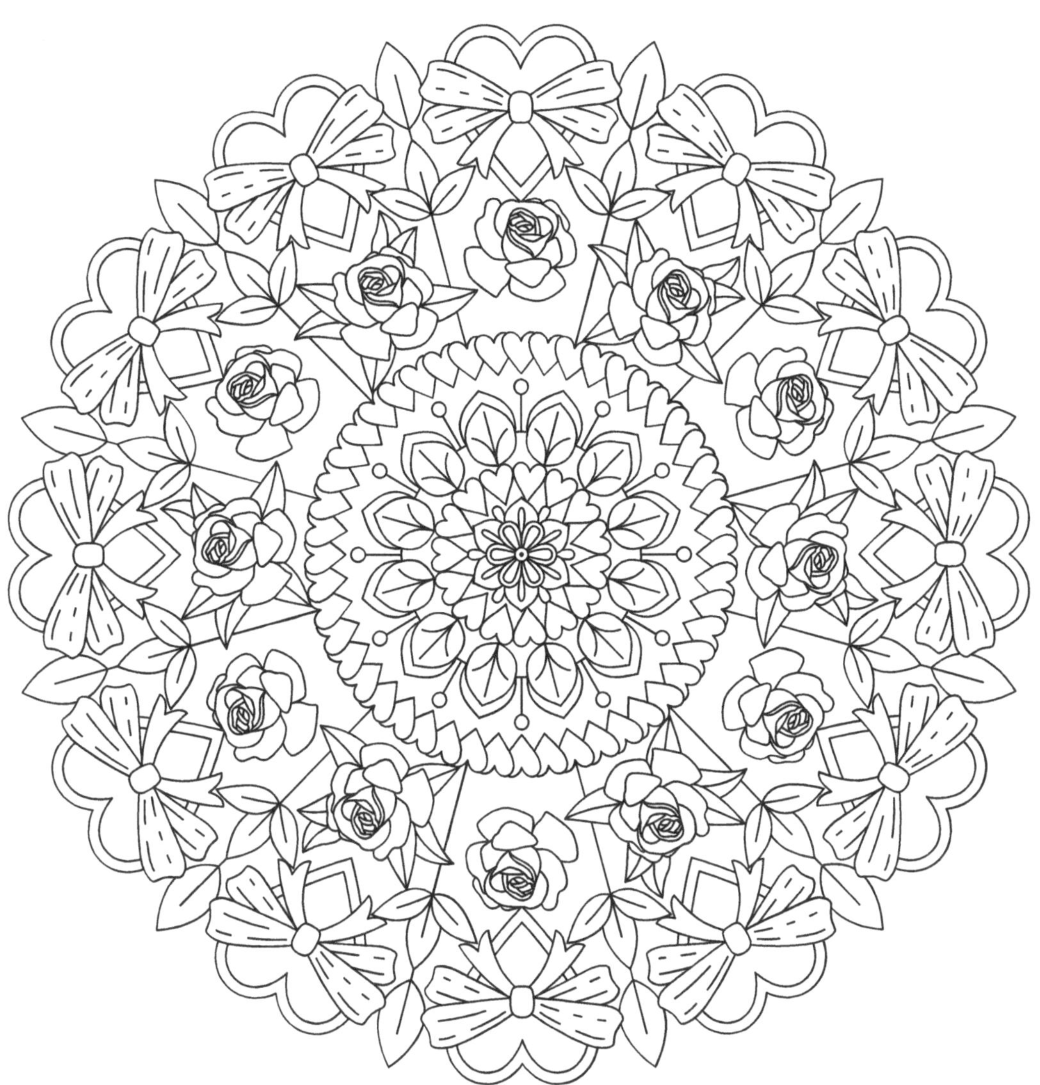

Belongs to

....

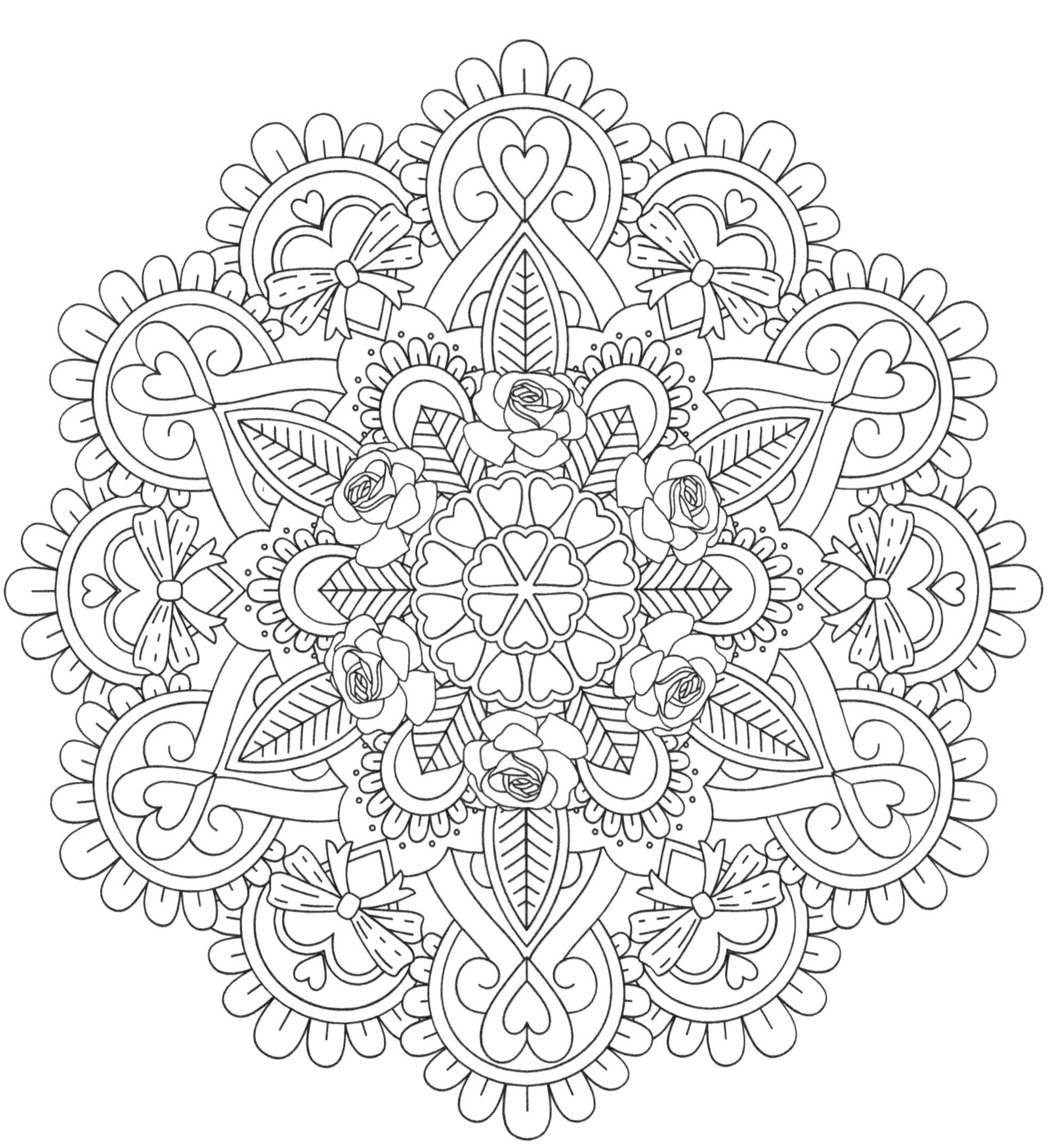

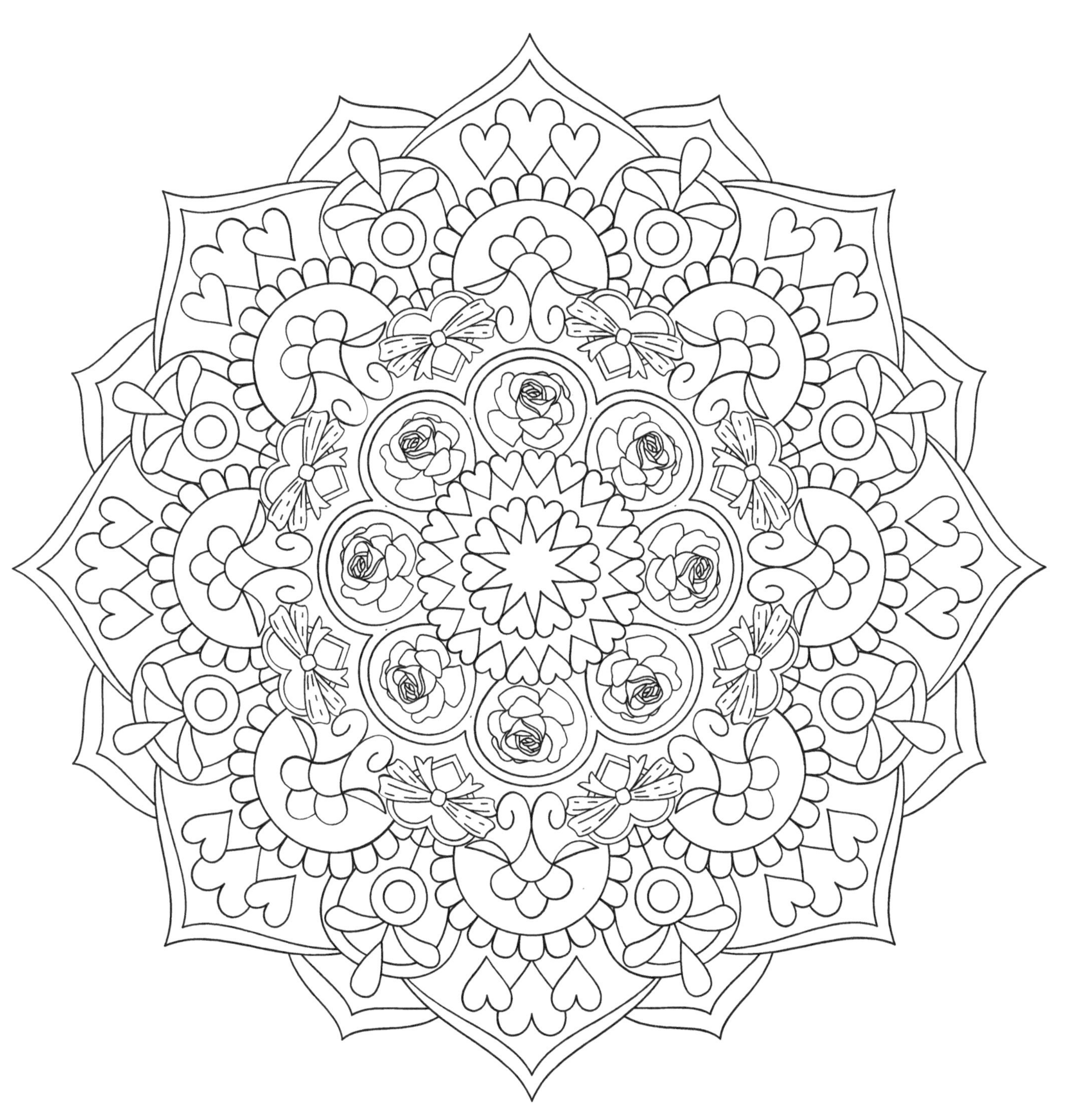

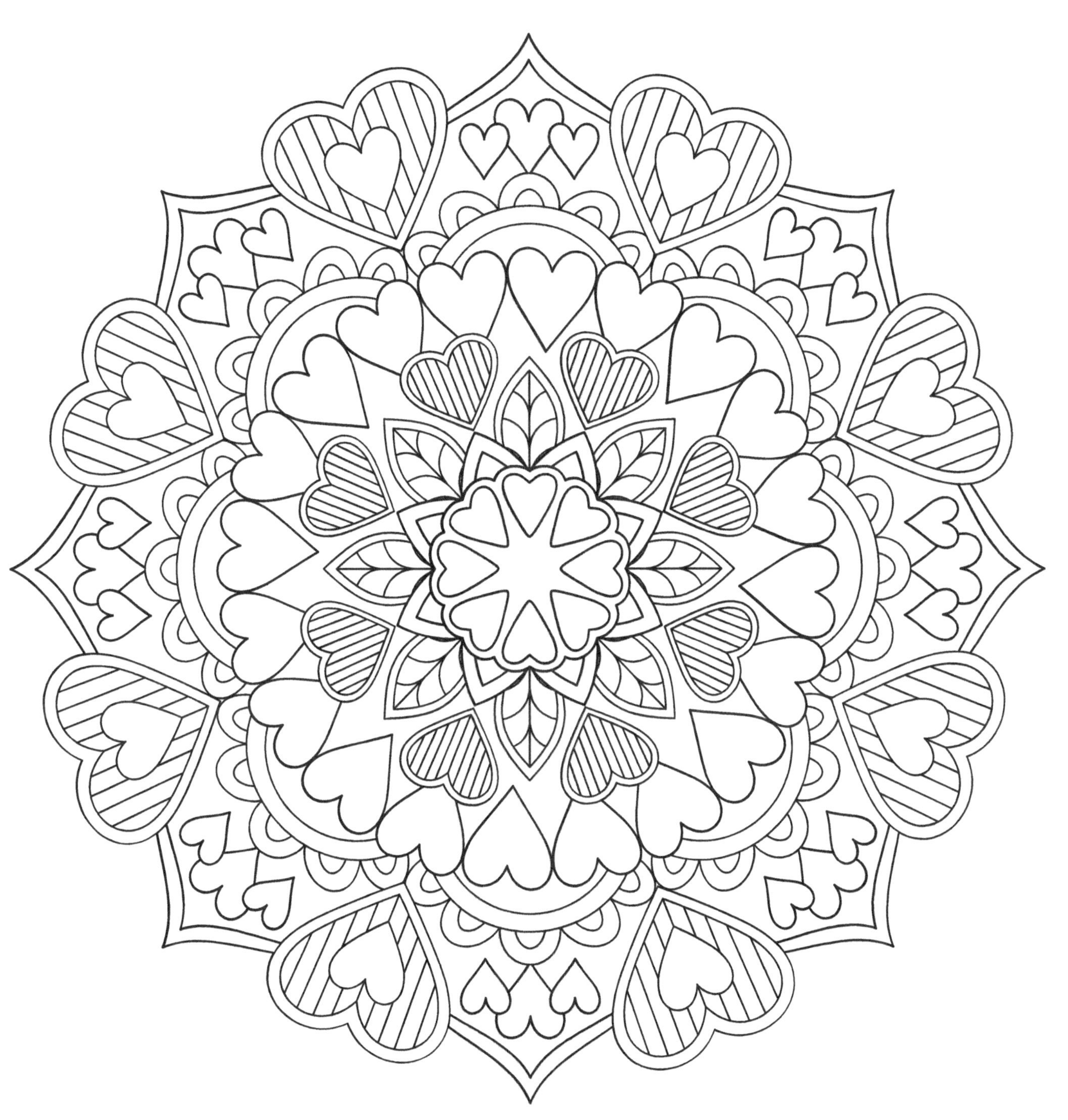

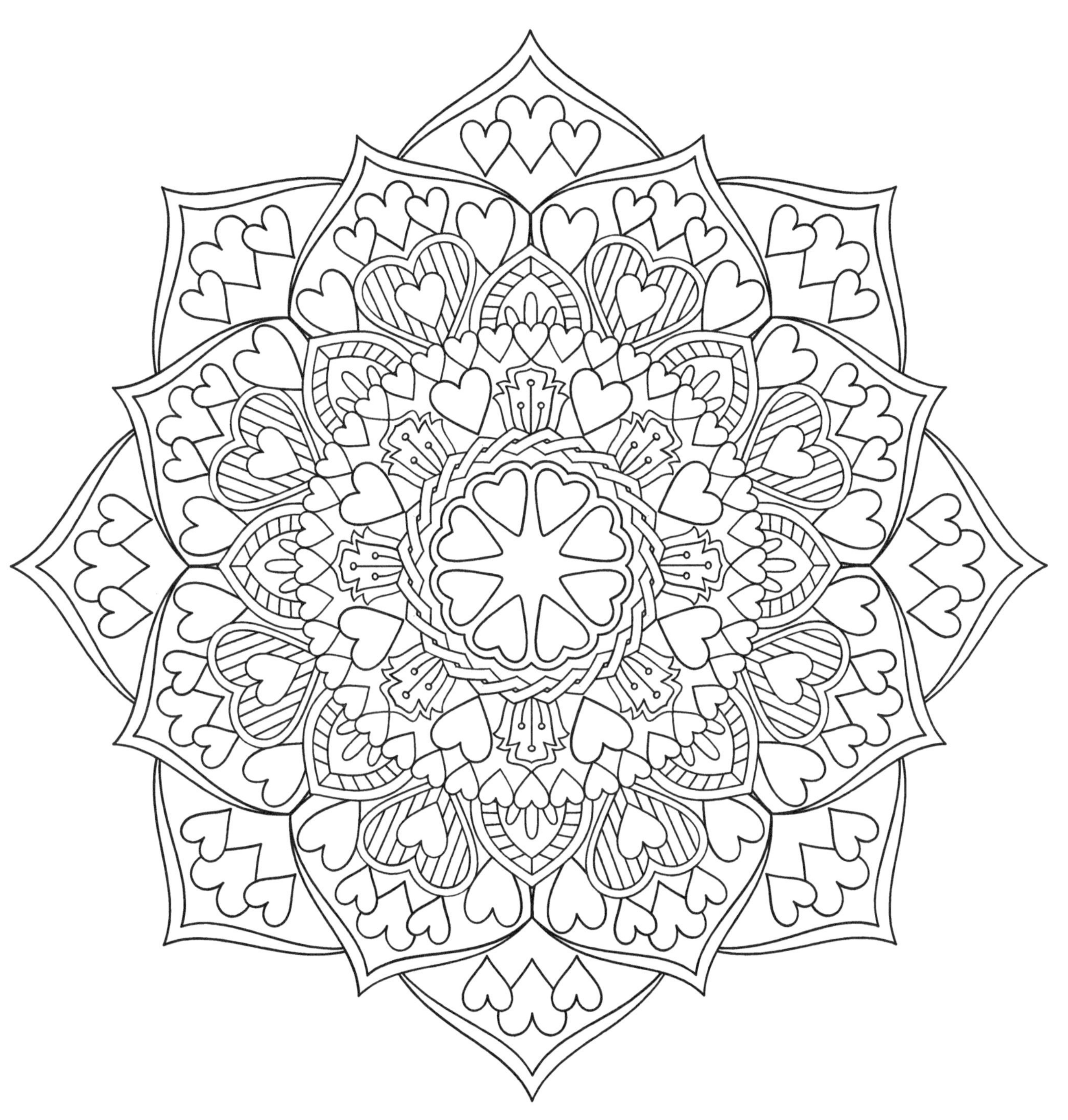

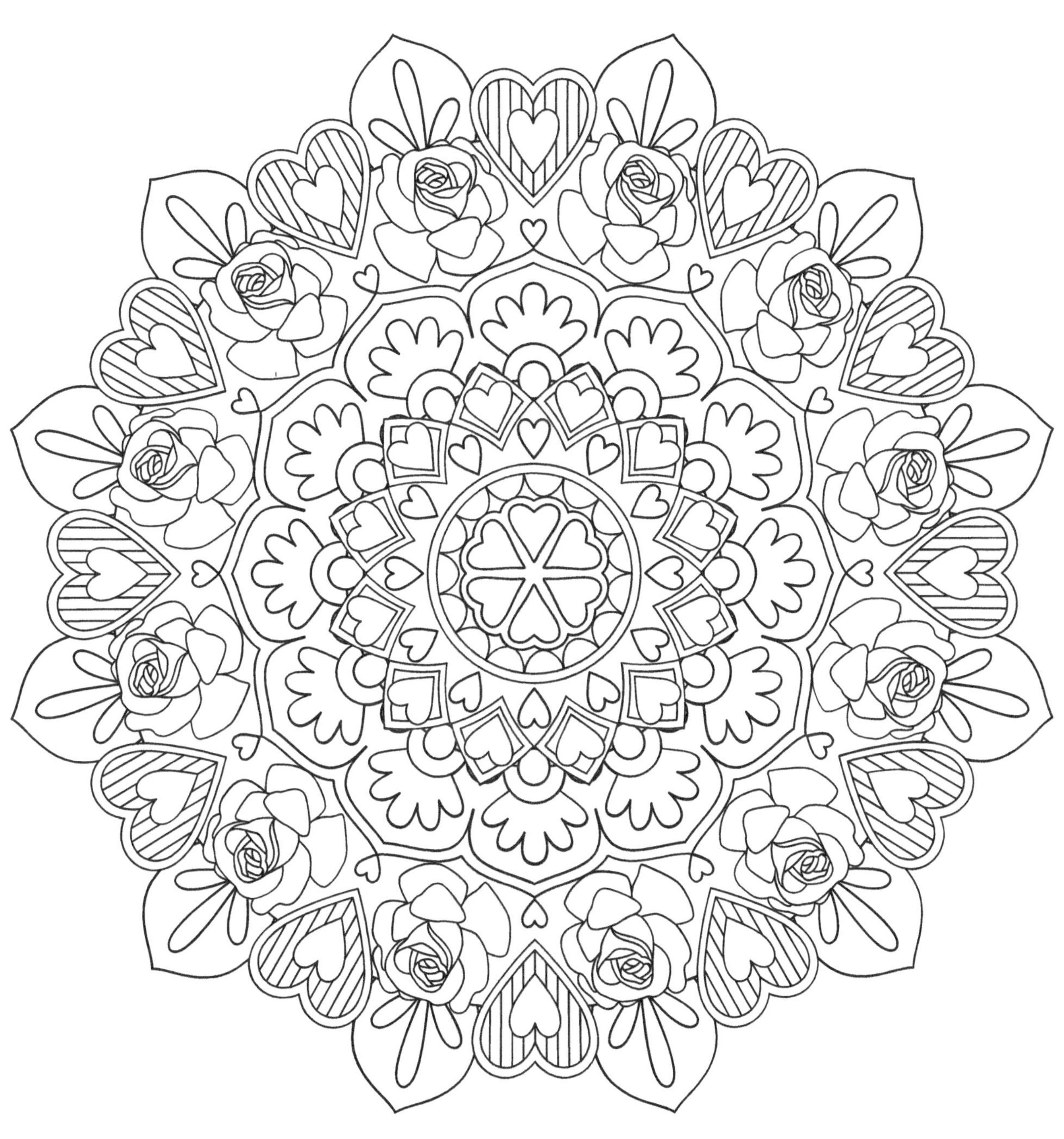

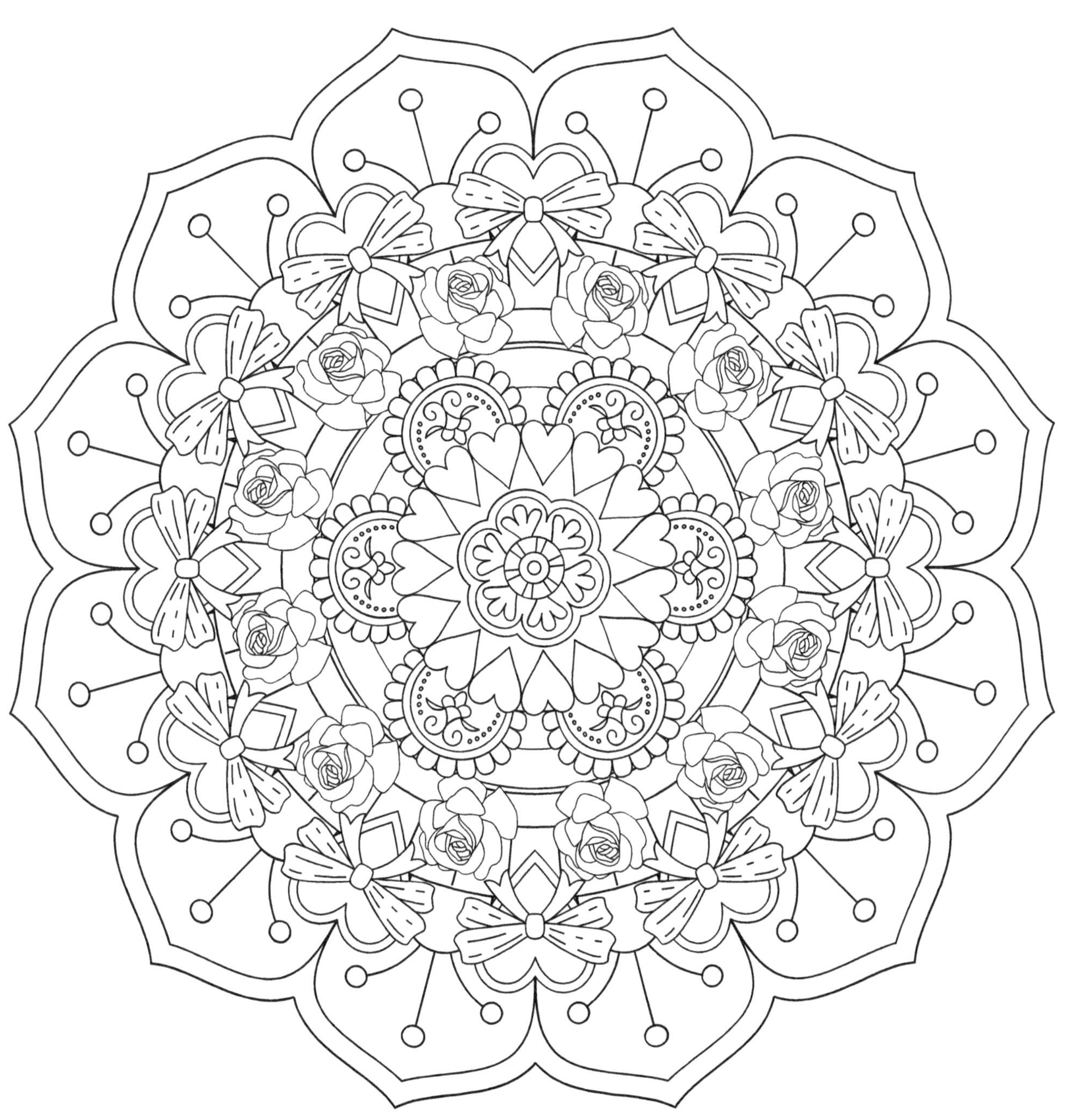

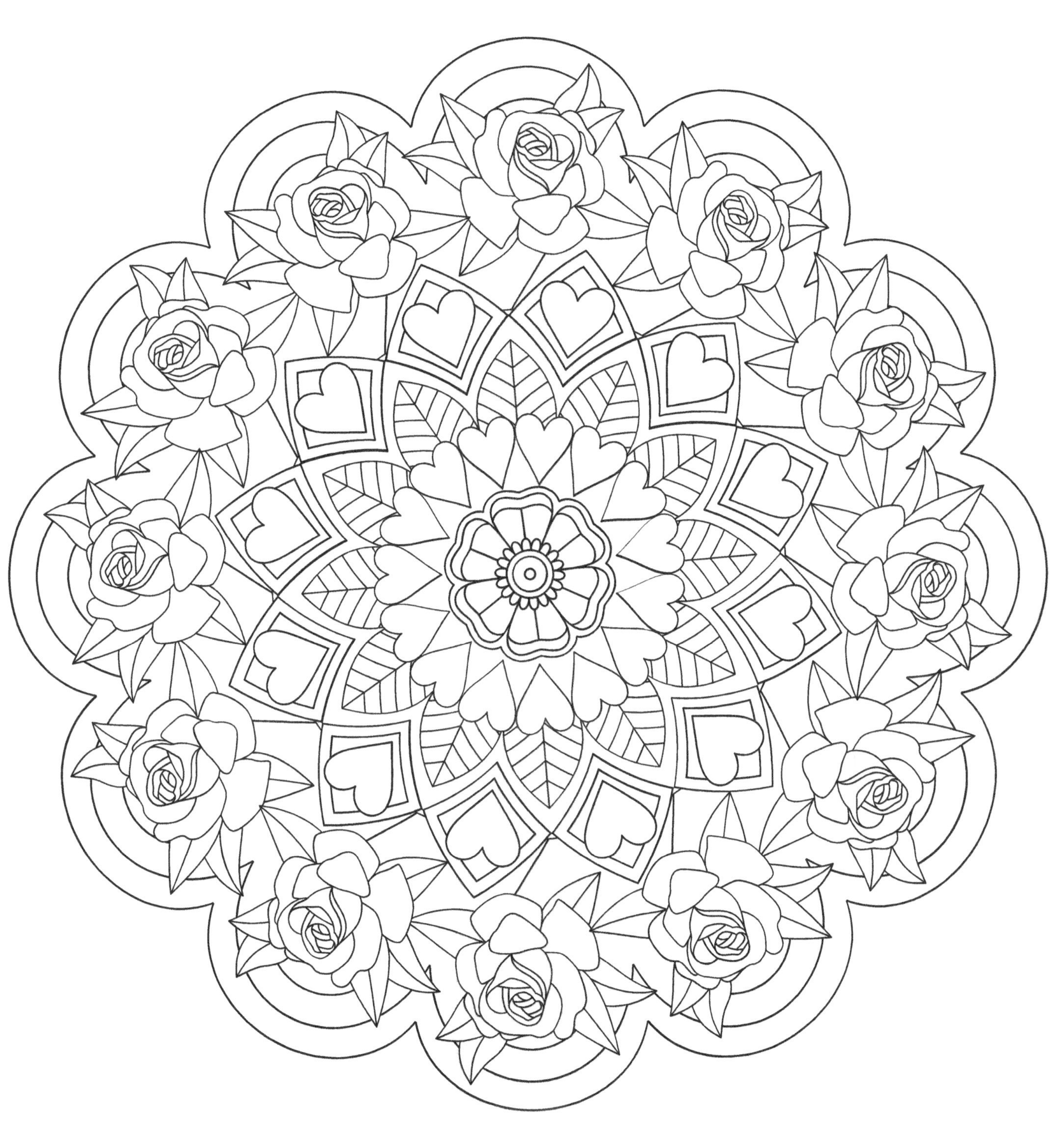

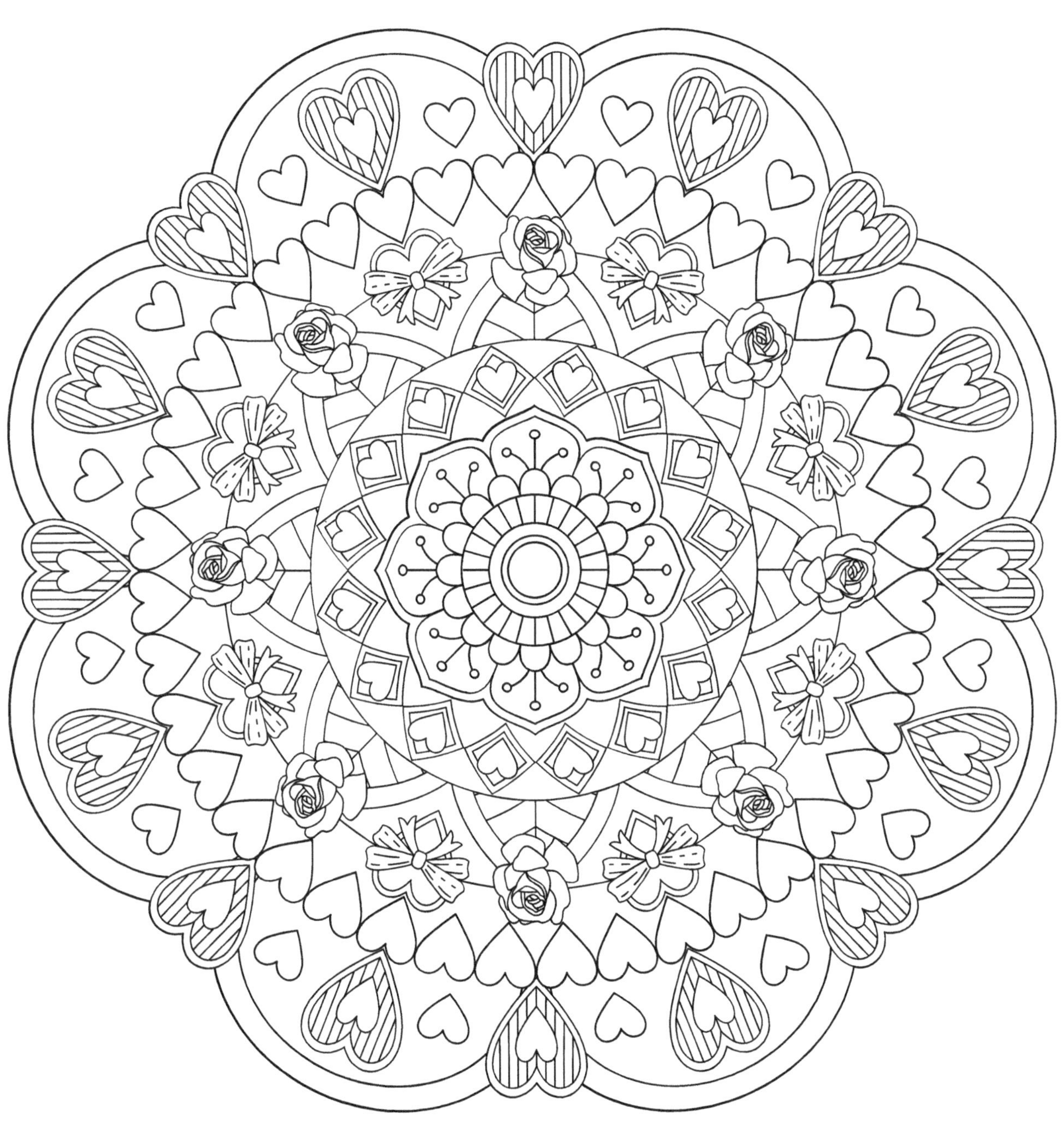

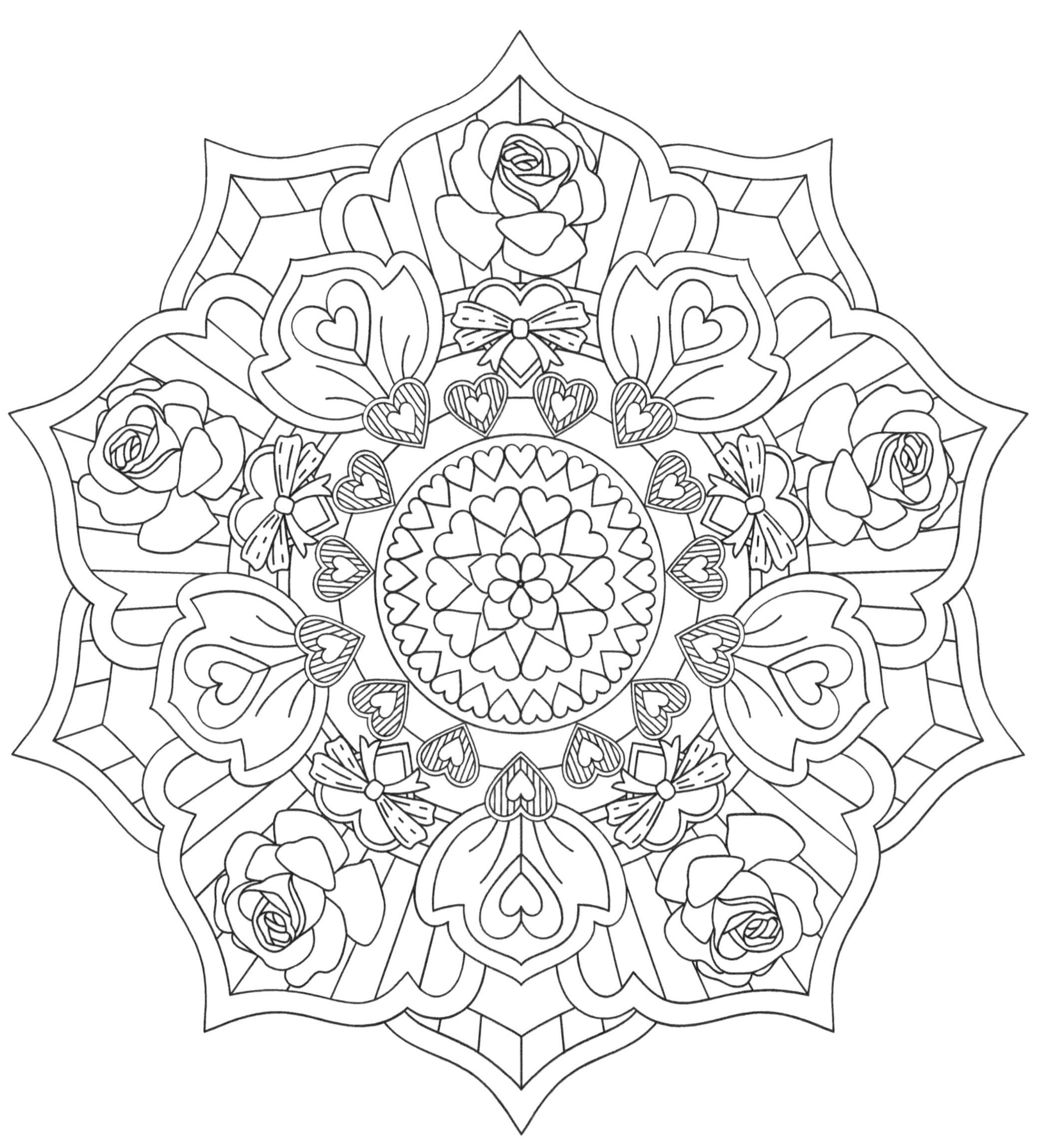

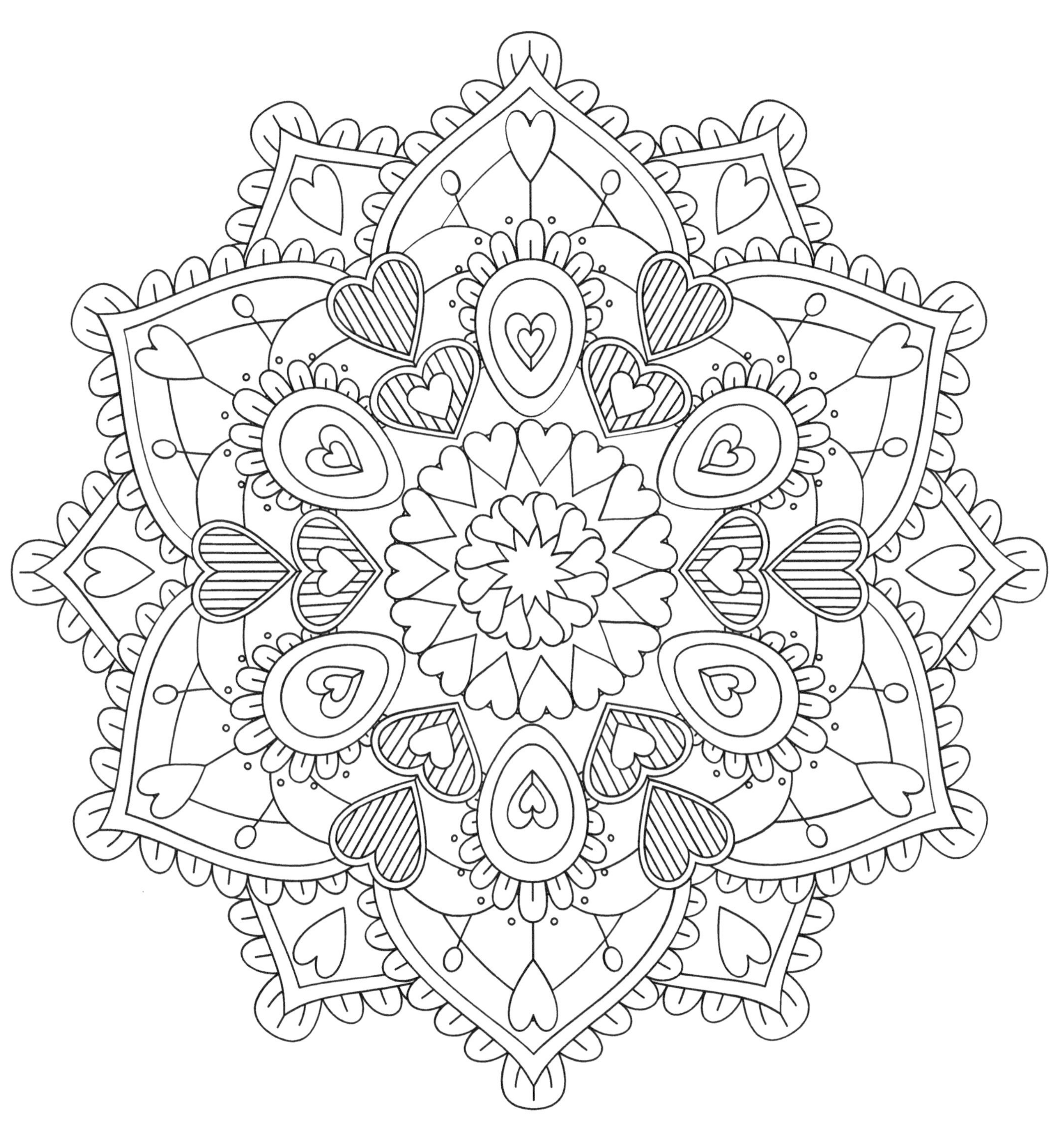

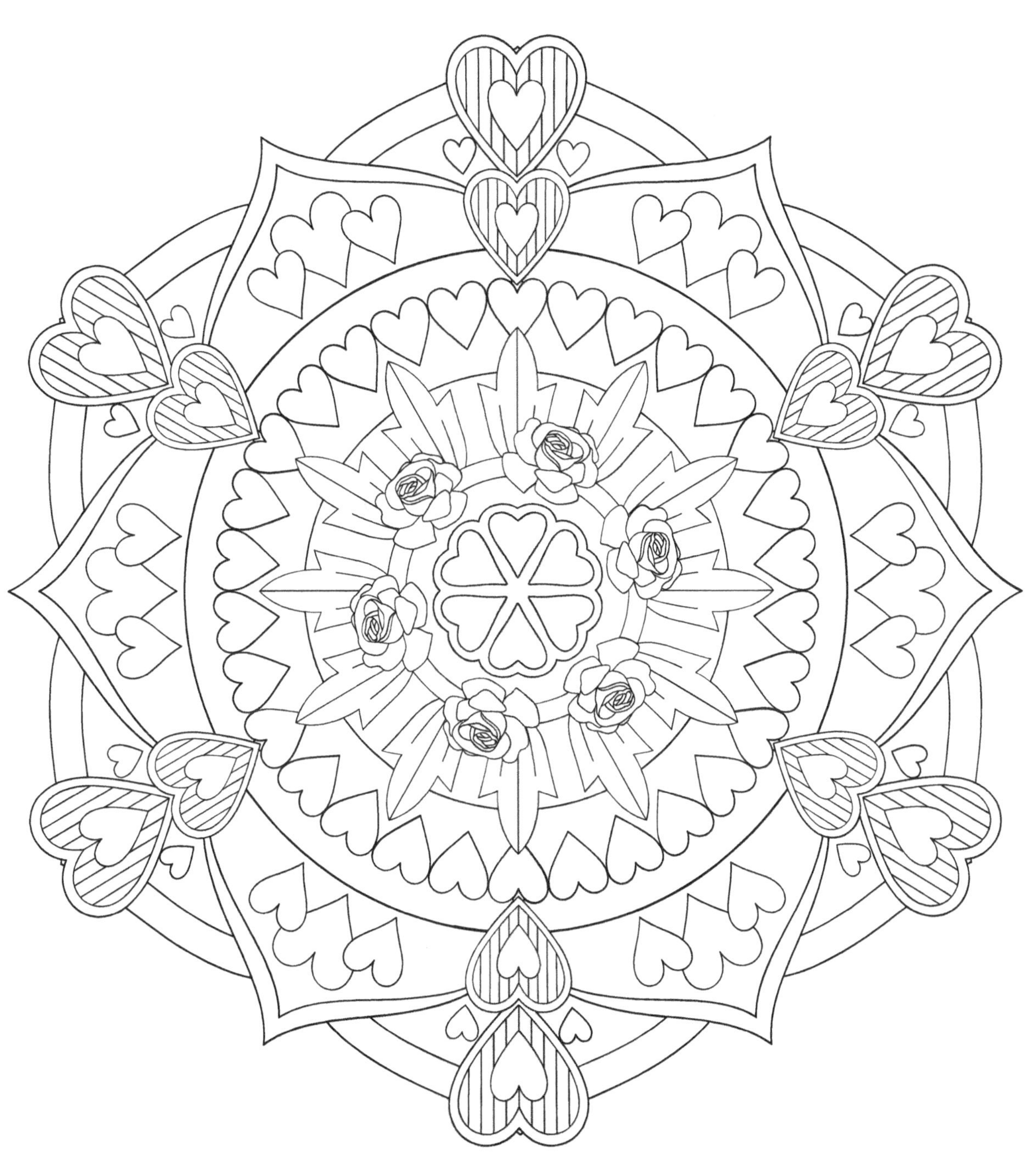

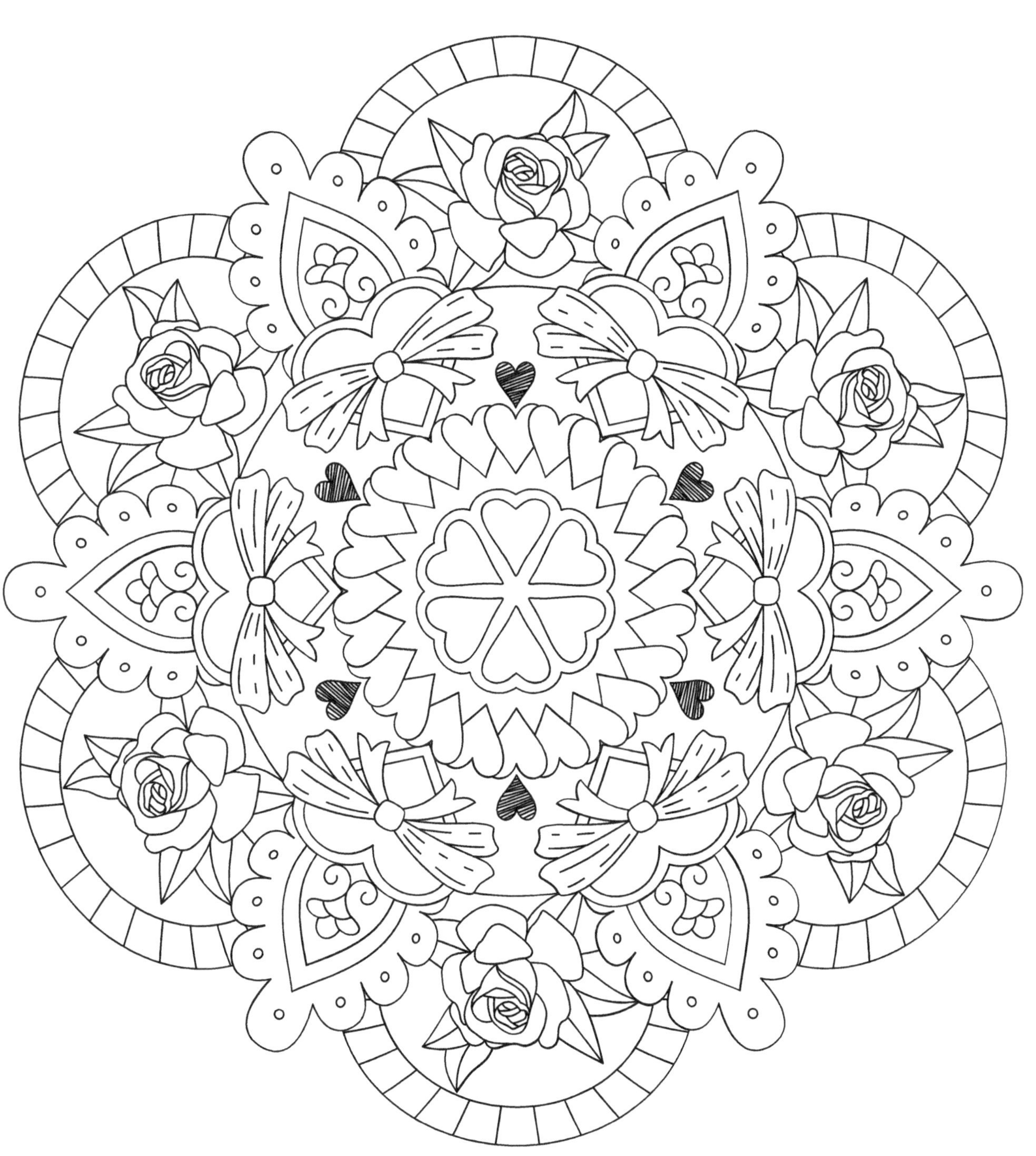

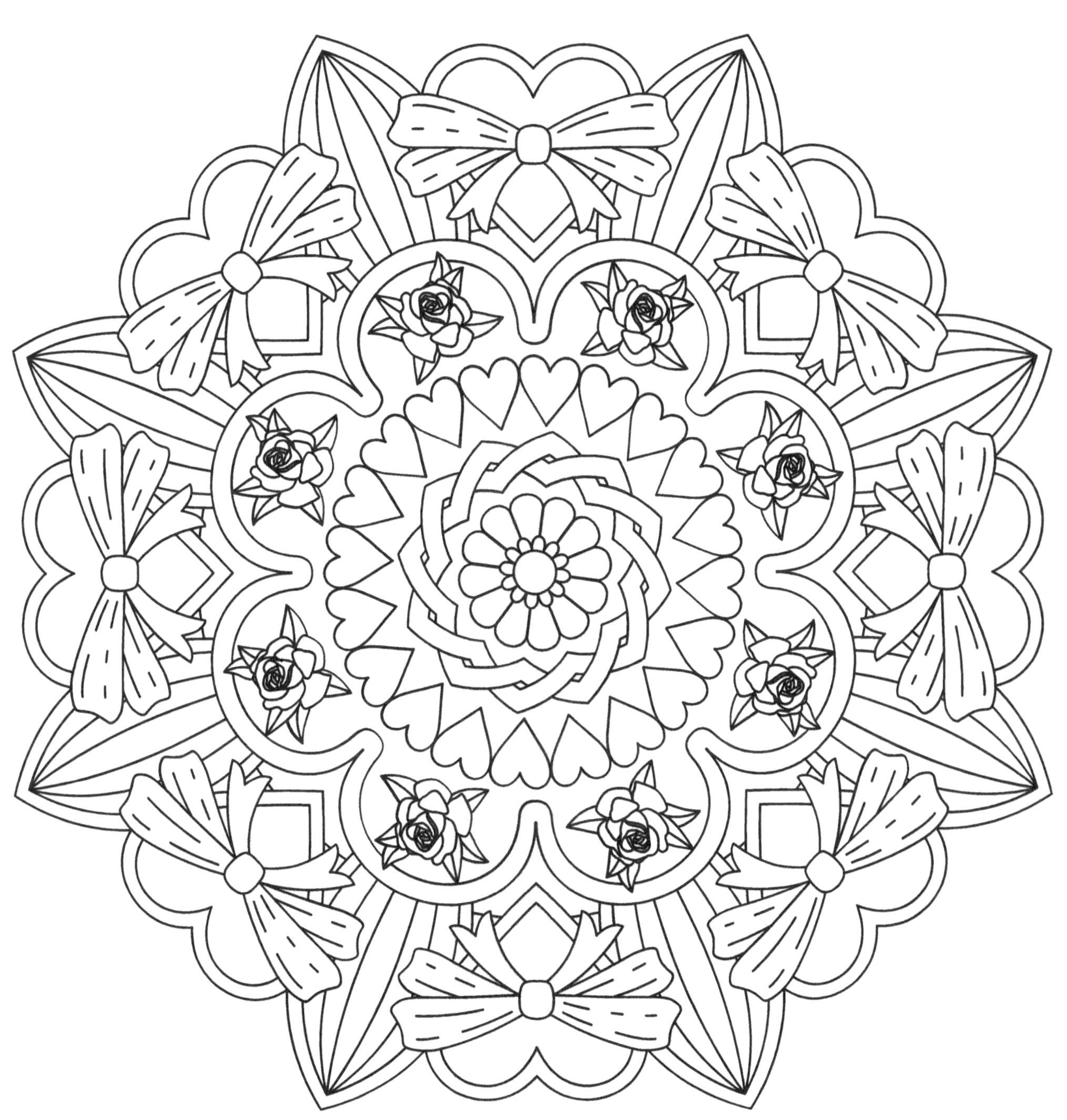

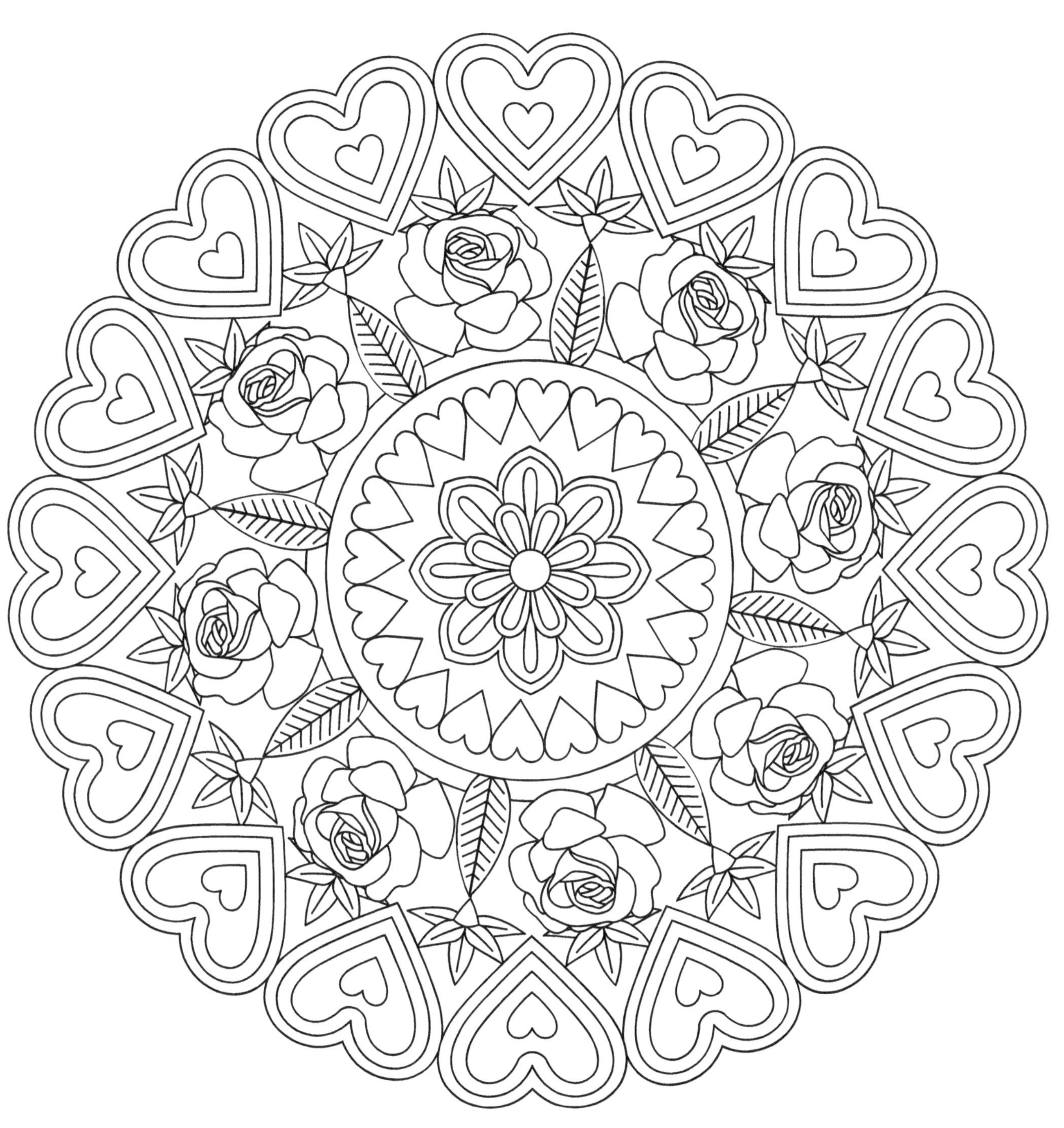

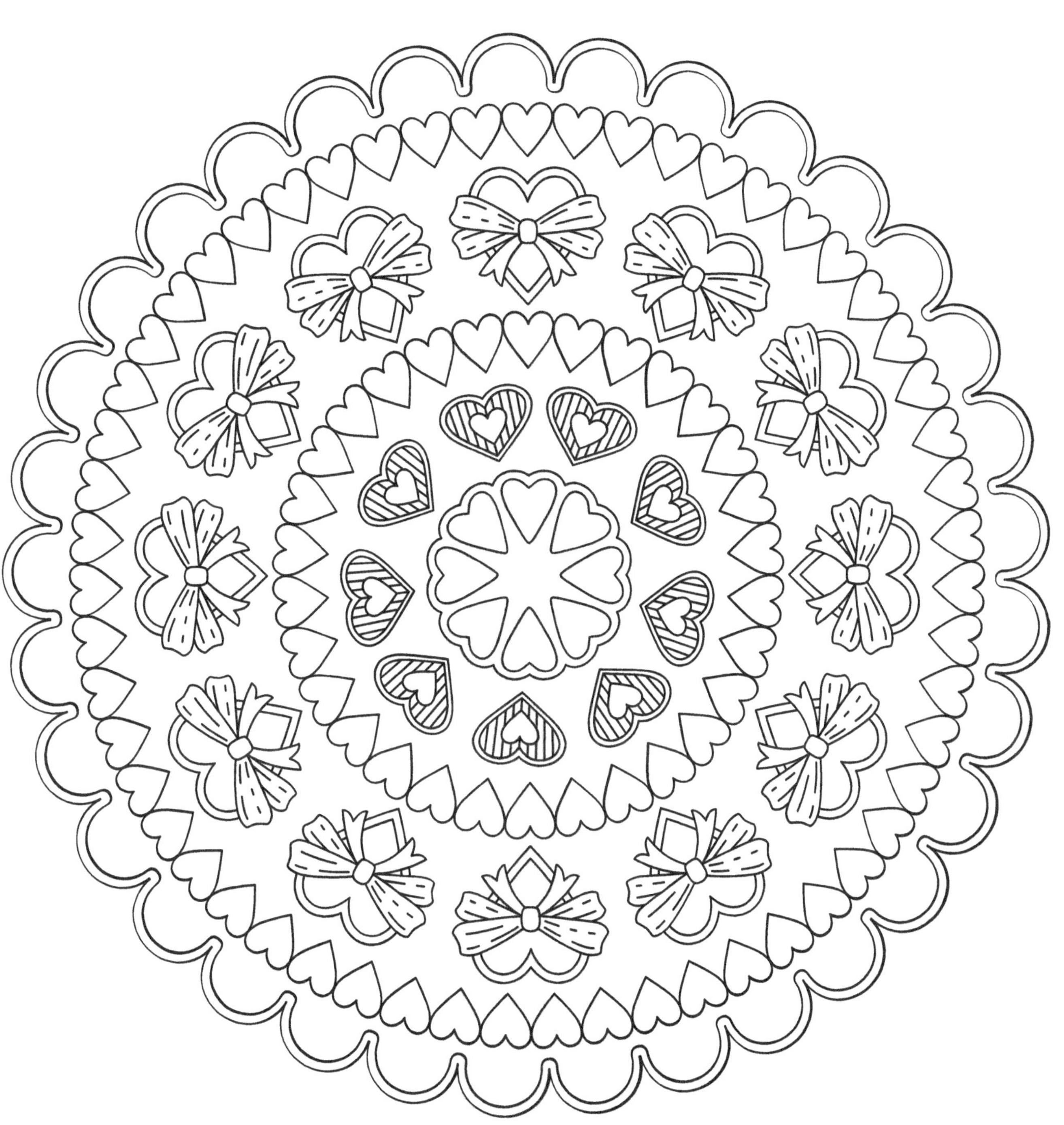

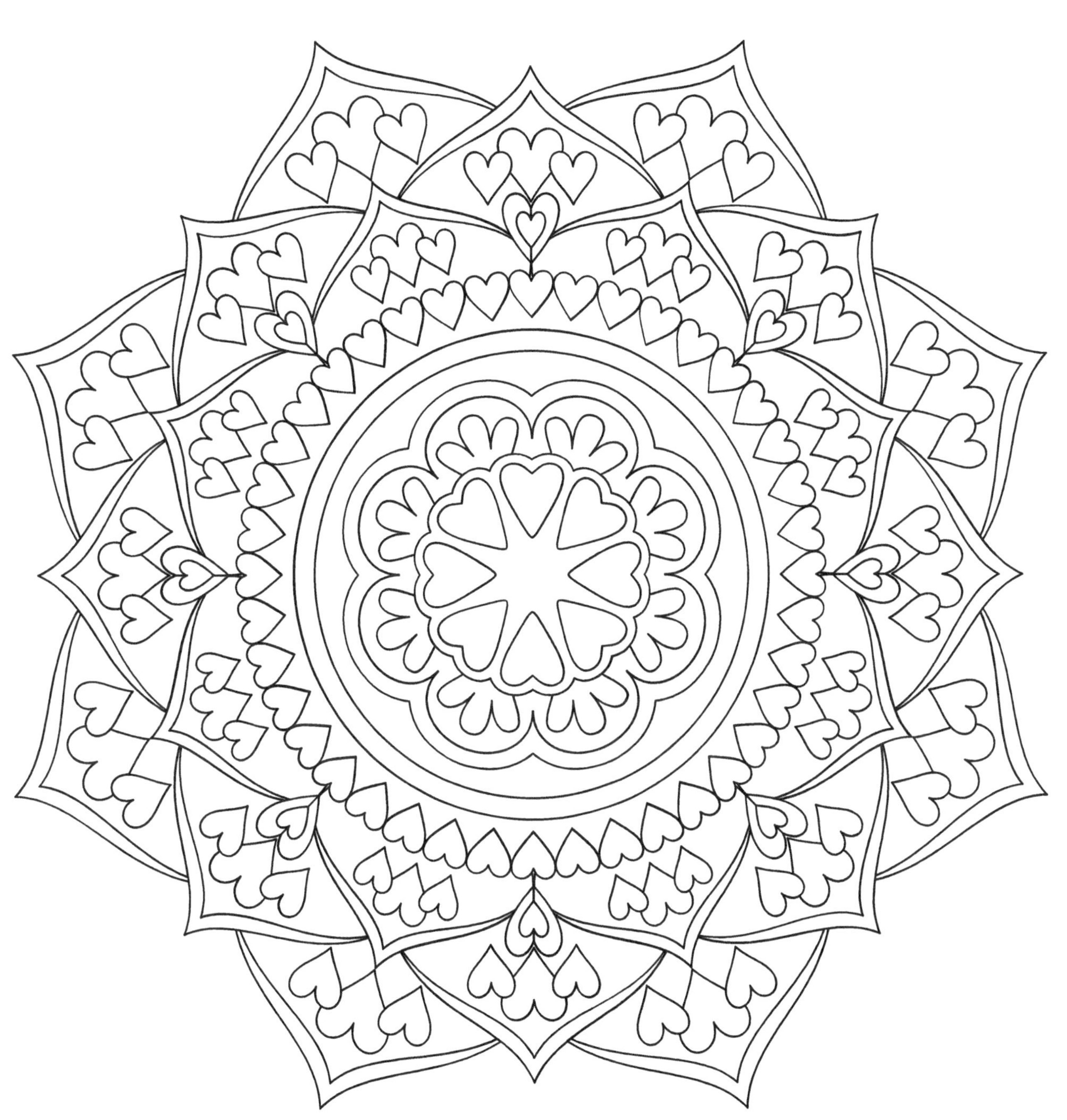

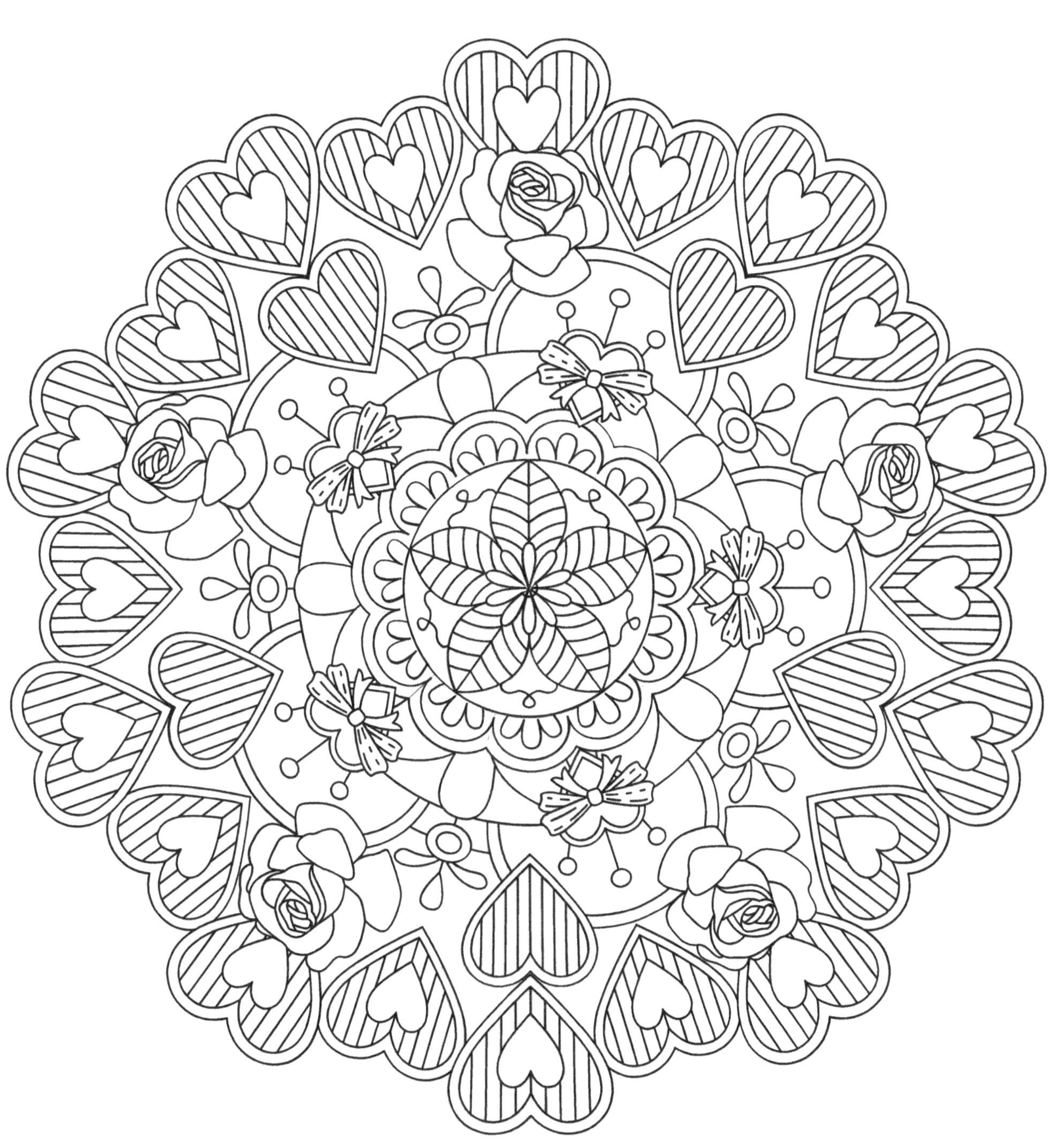

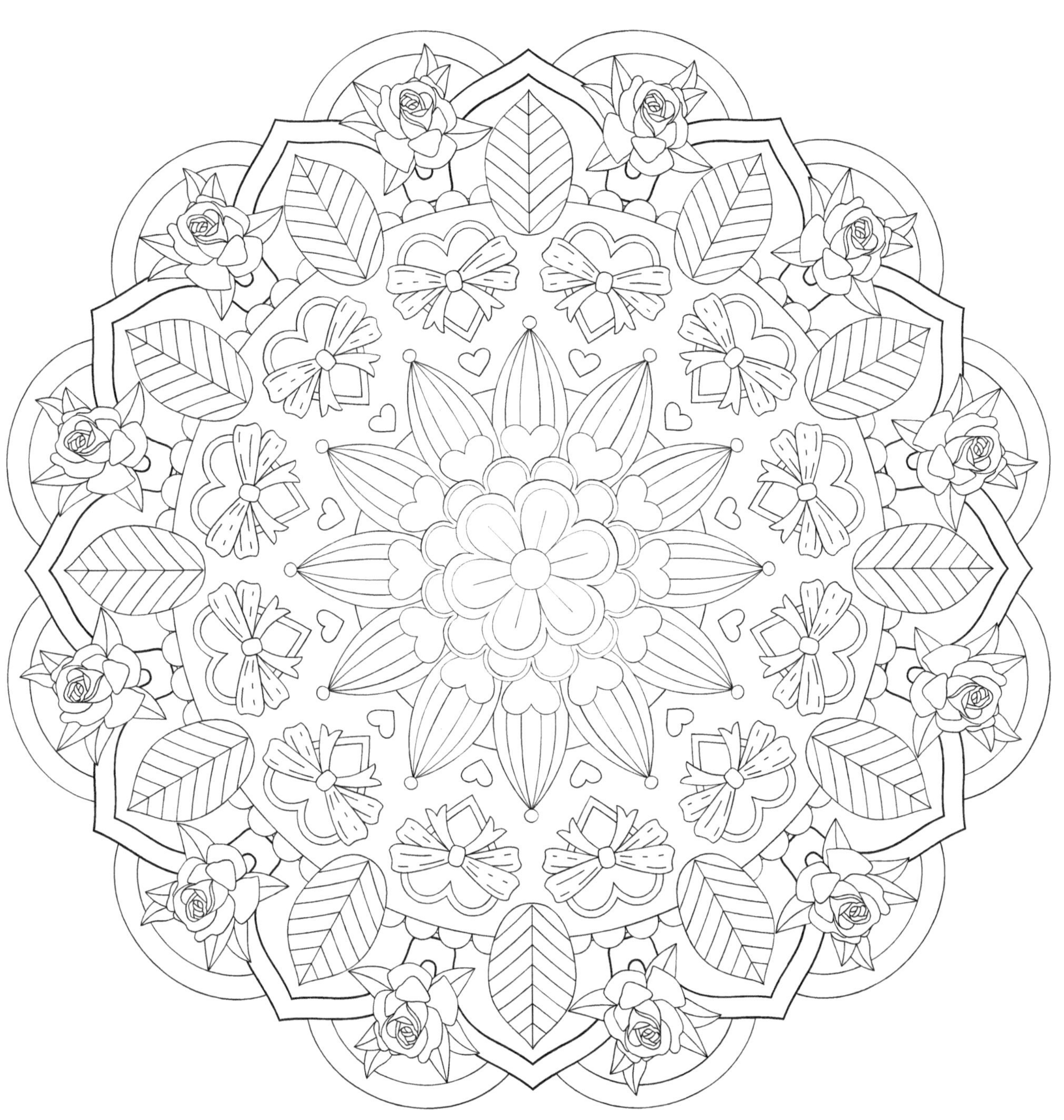

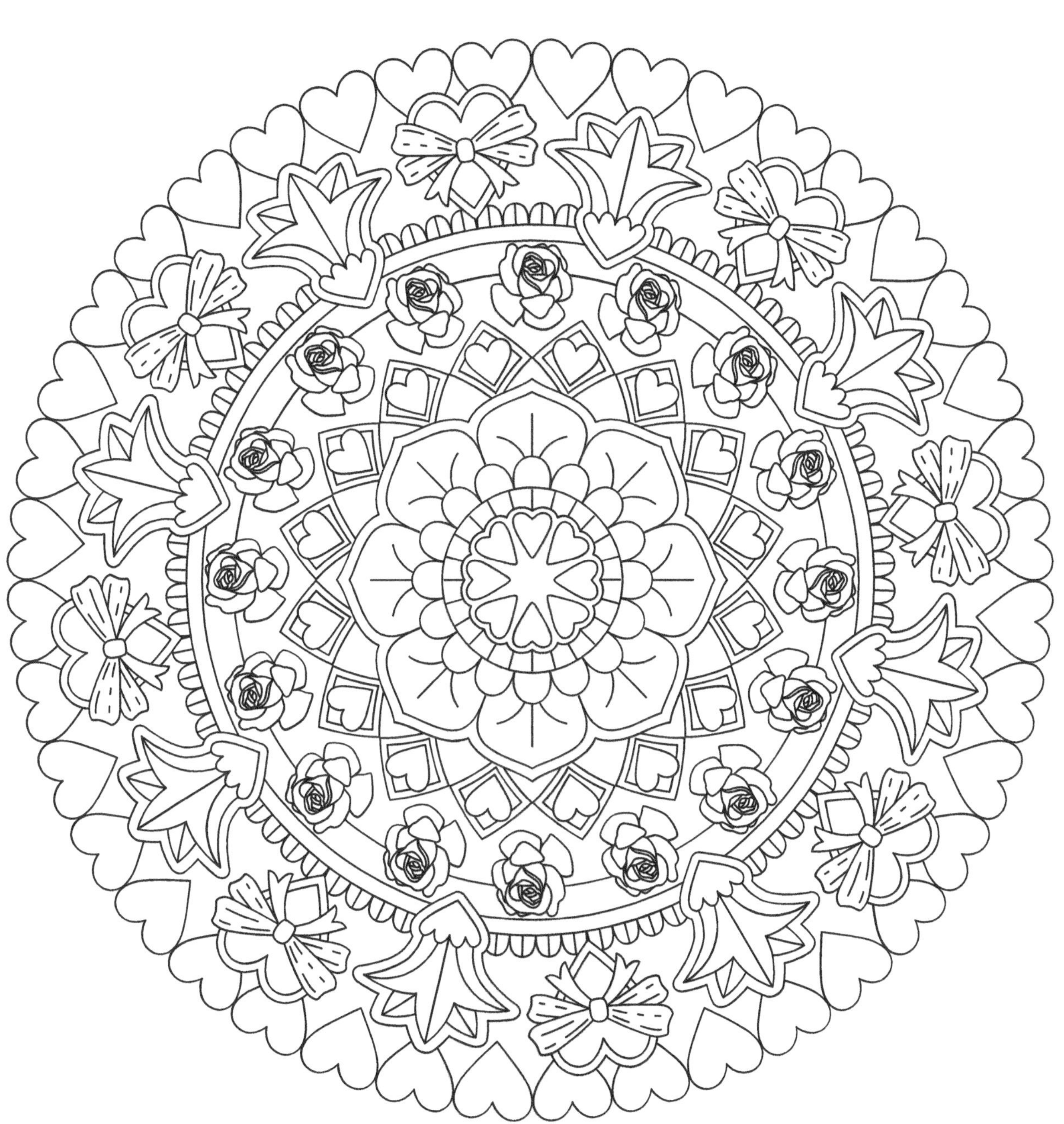

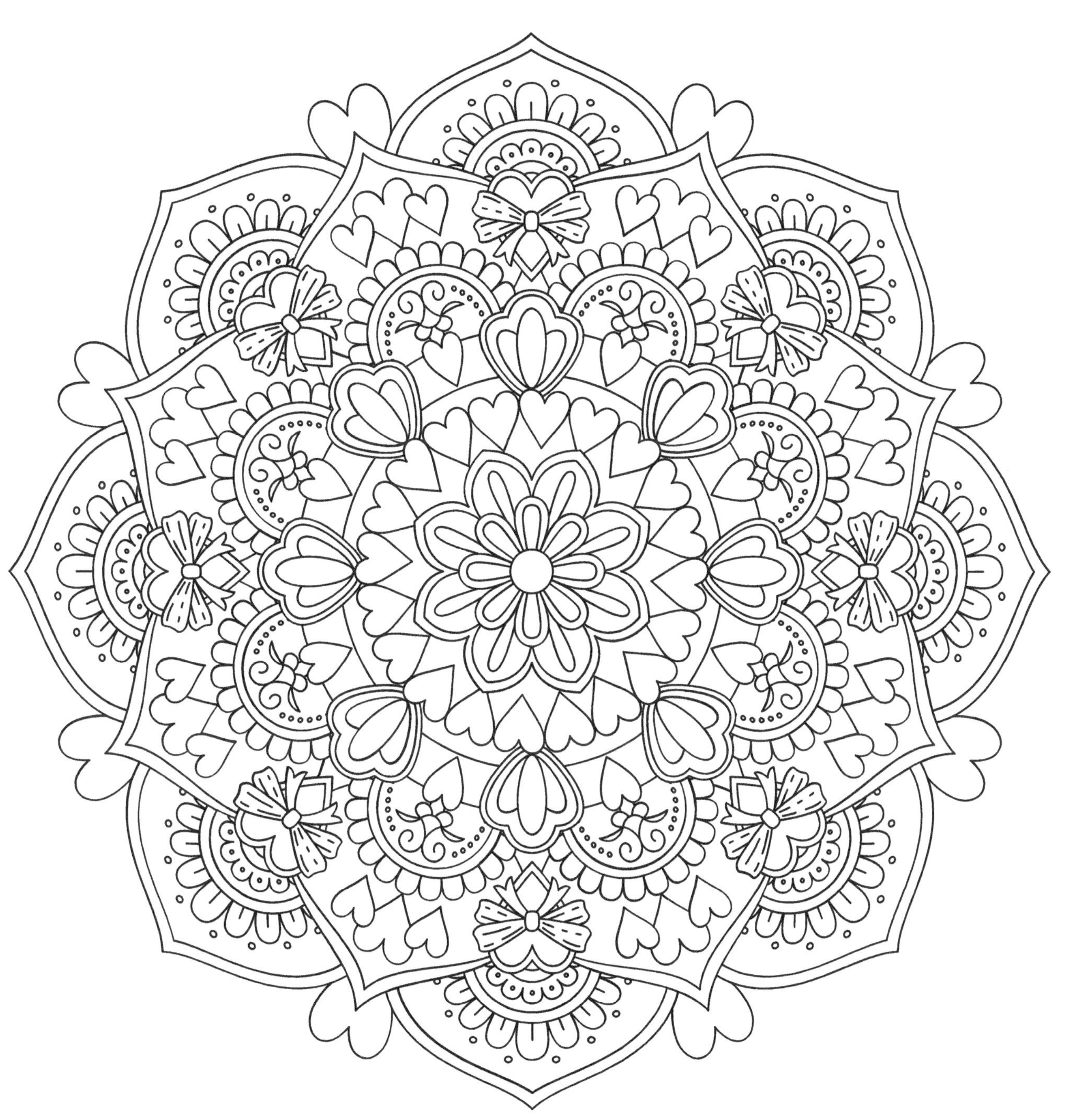

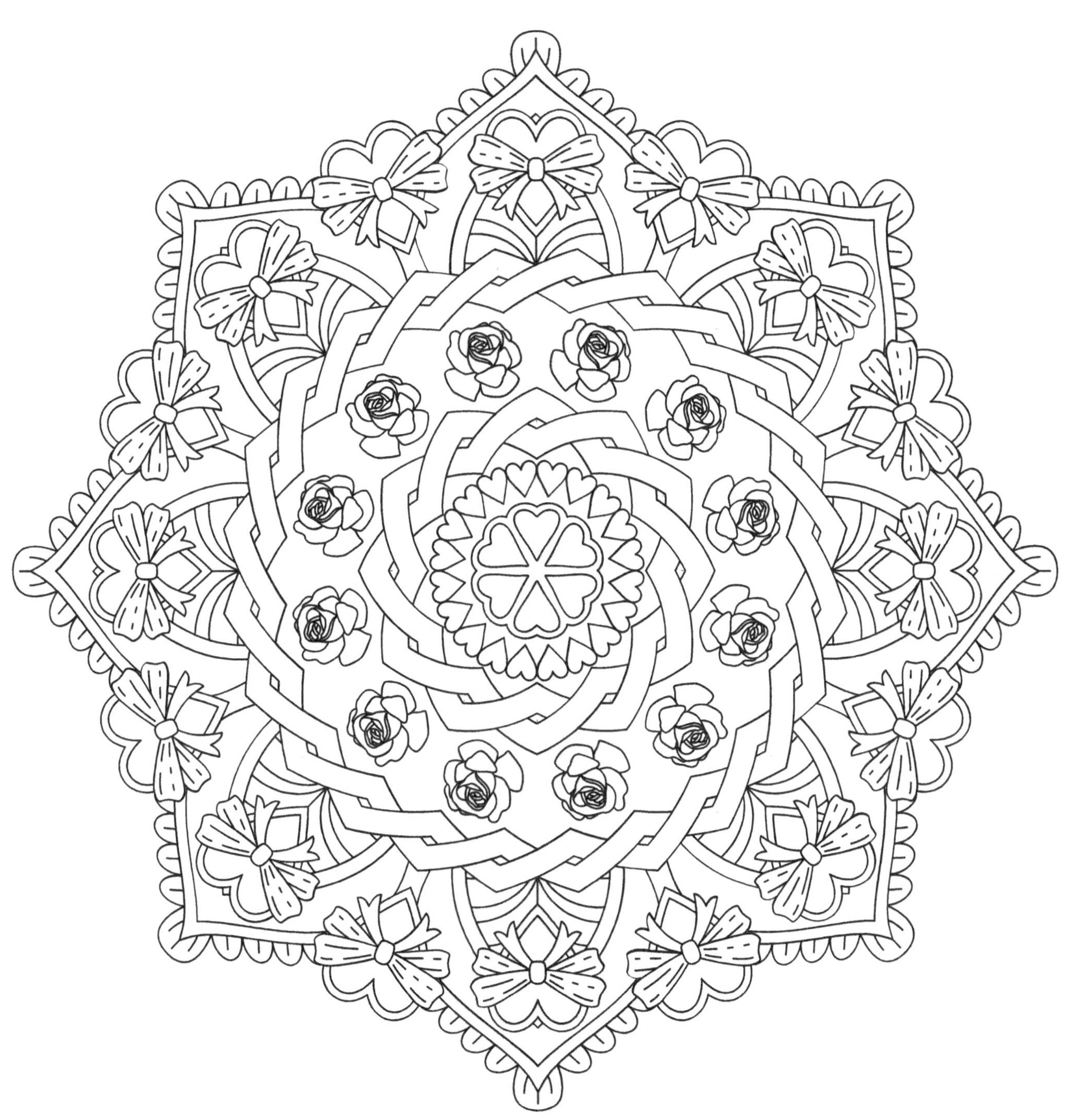

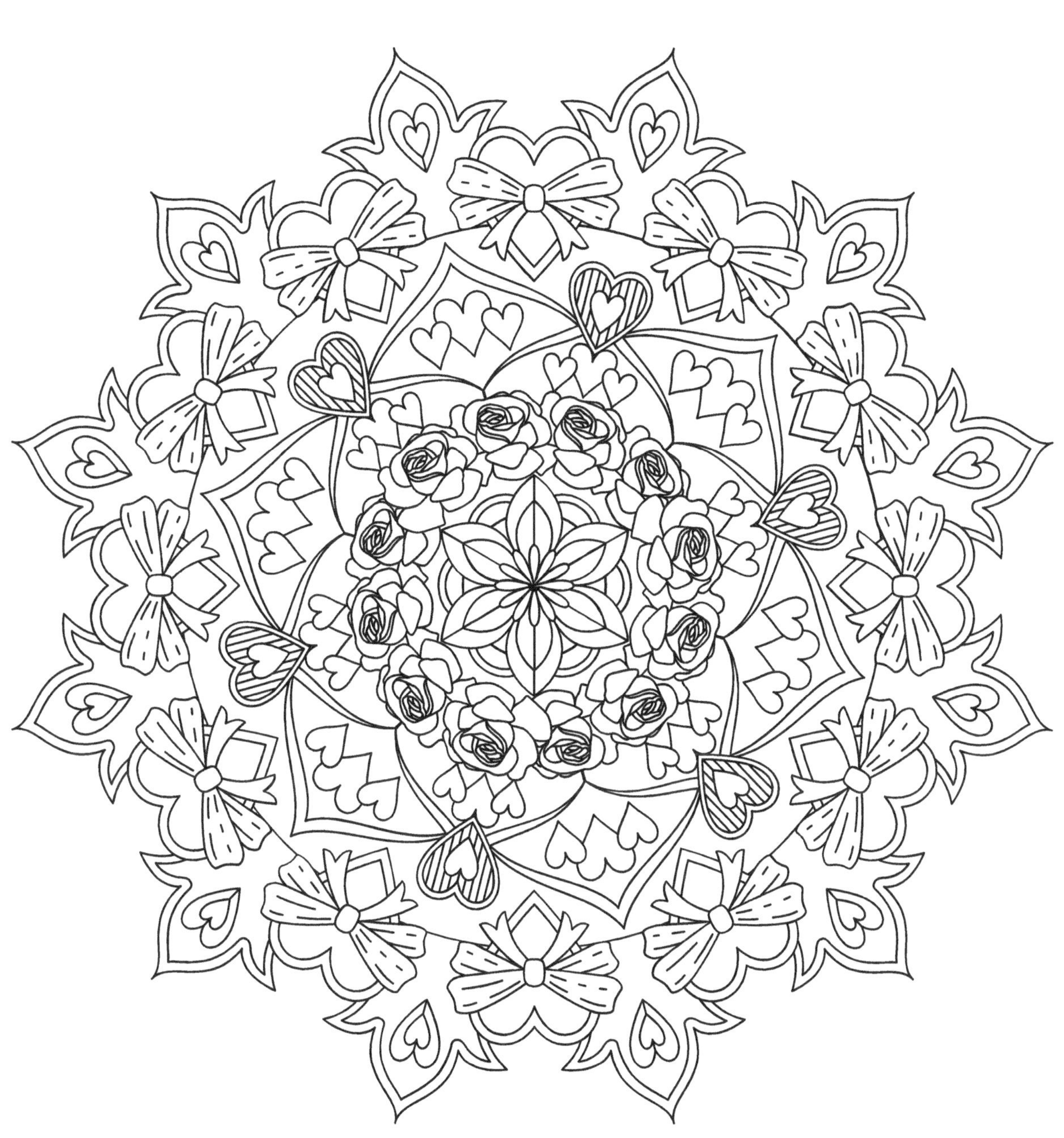

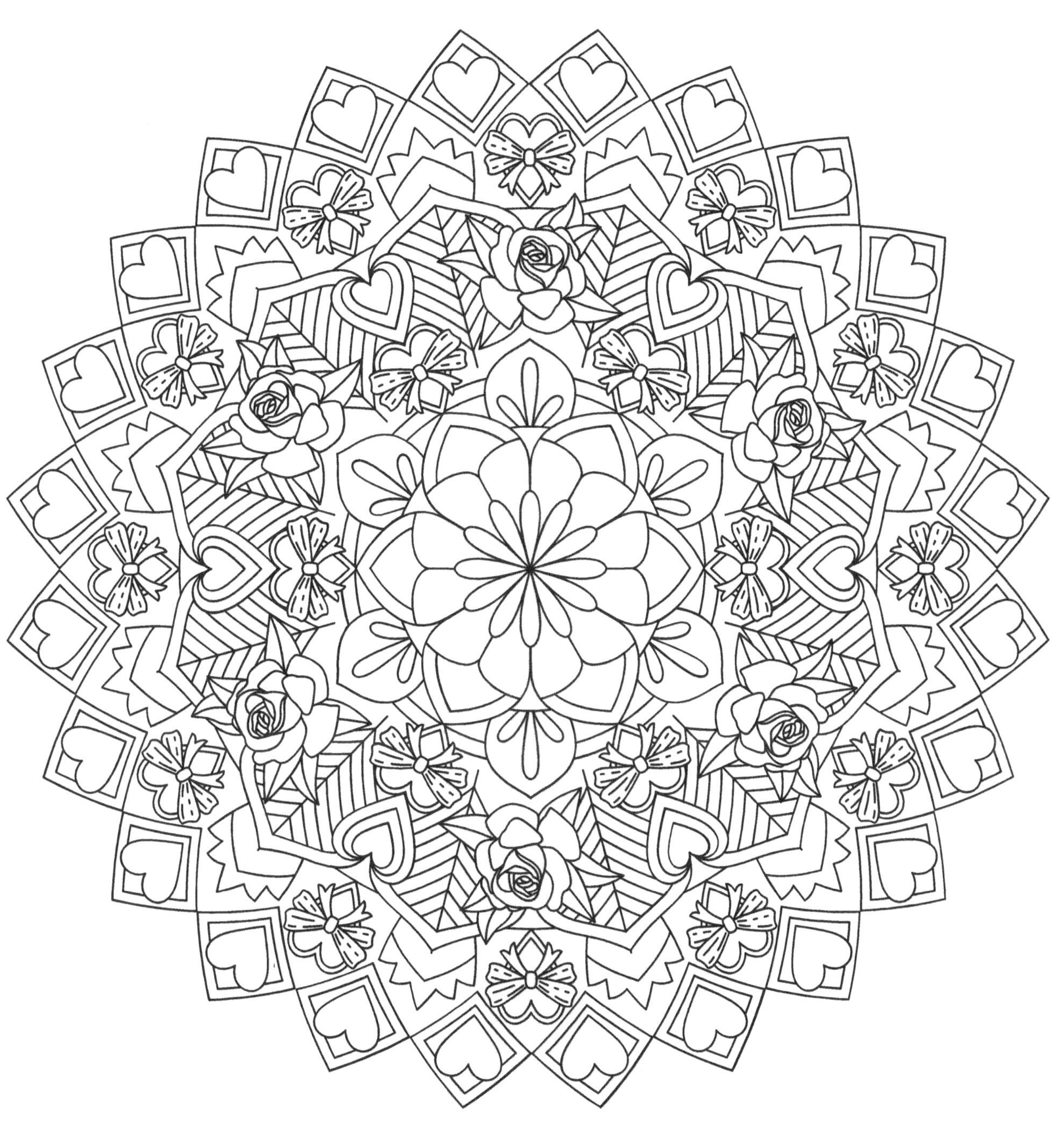

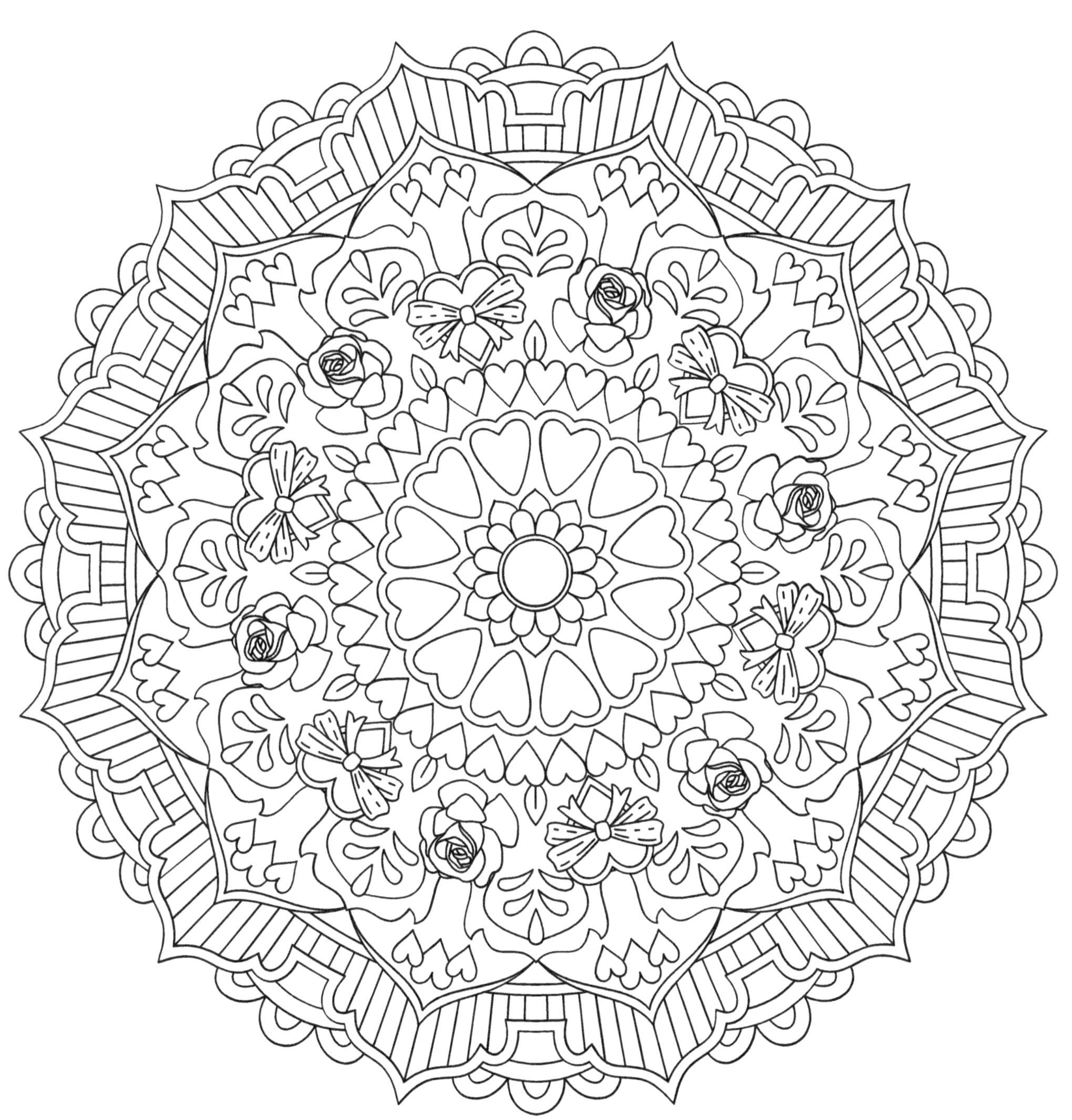

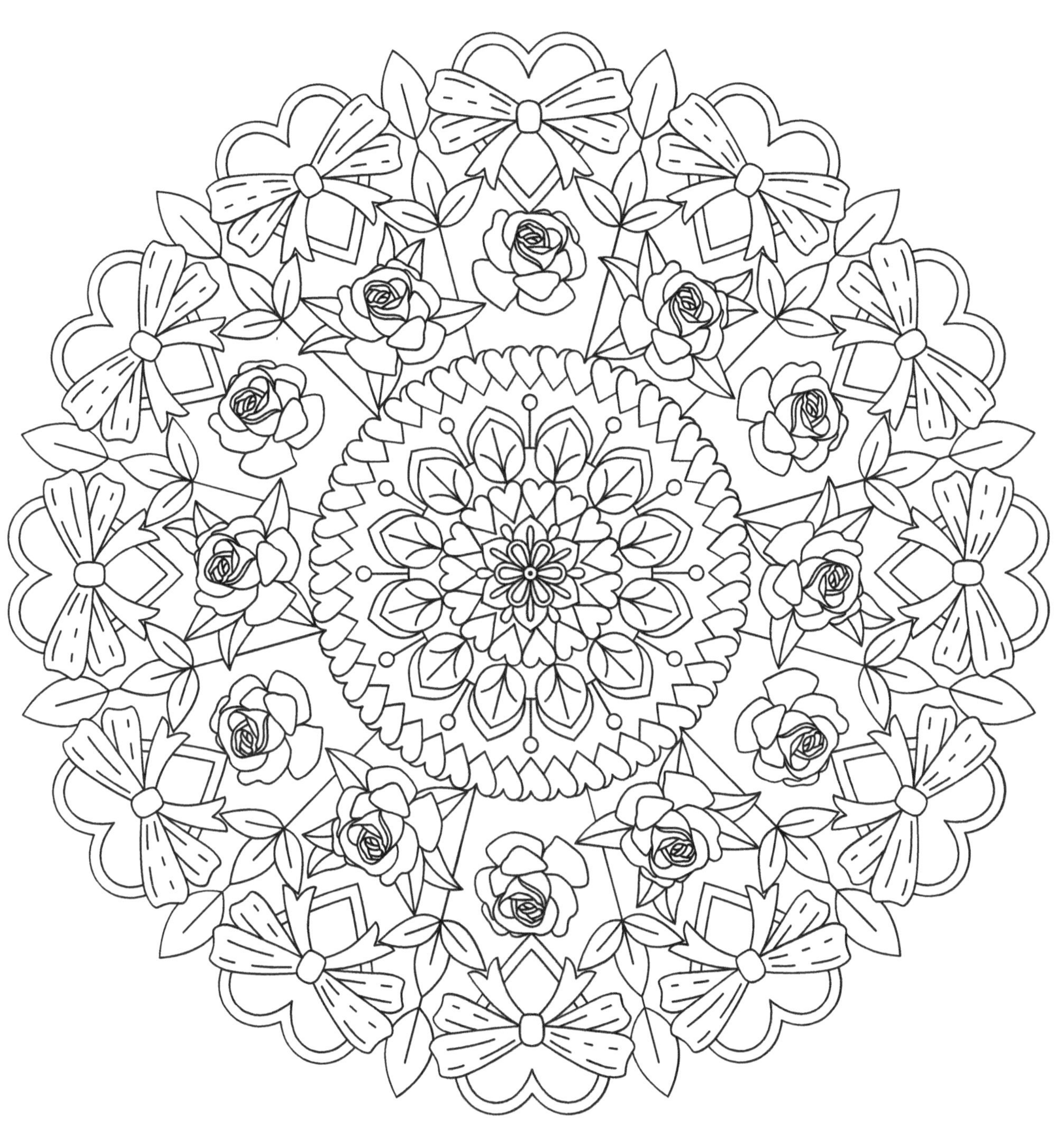

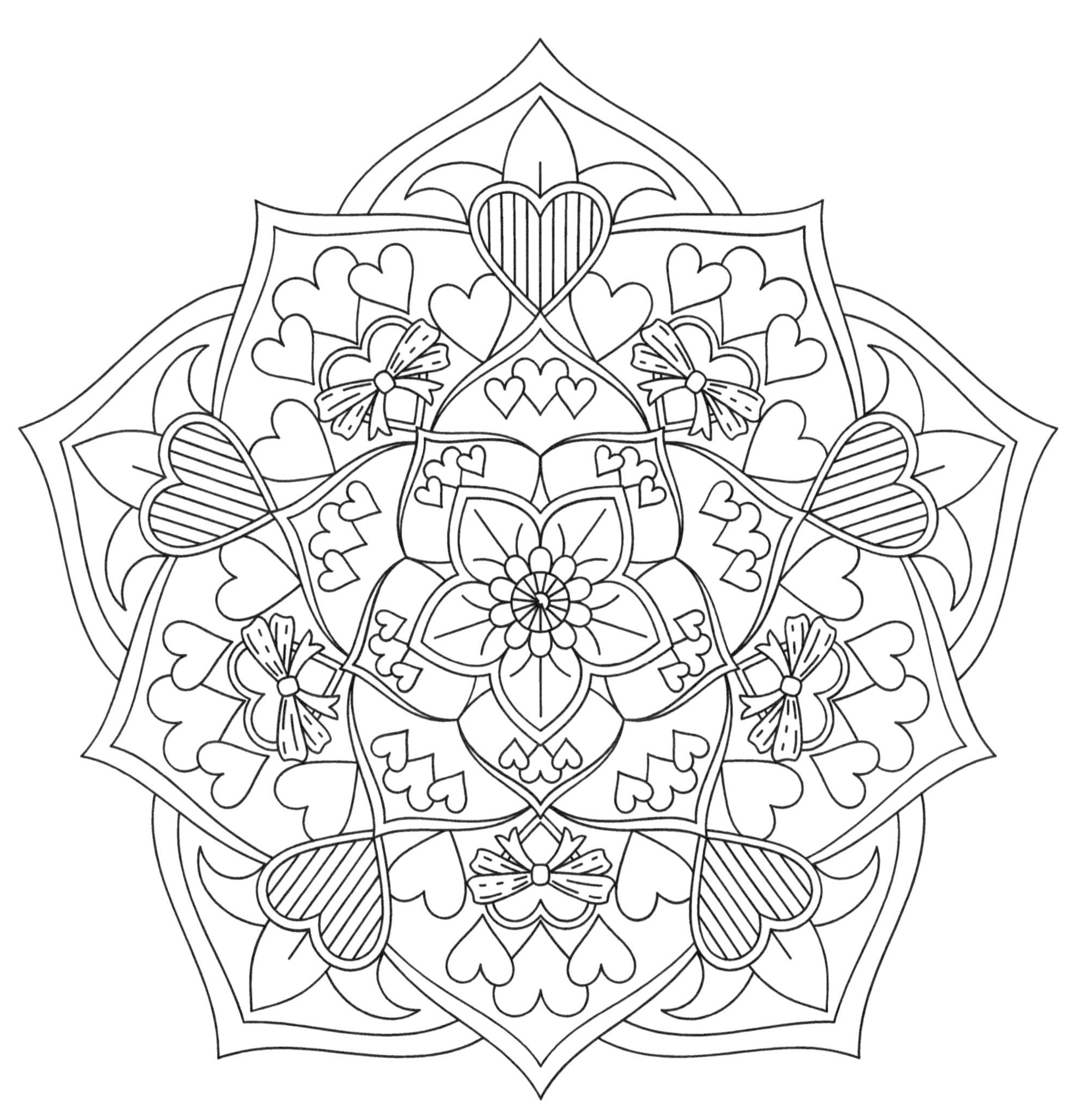

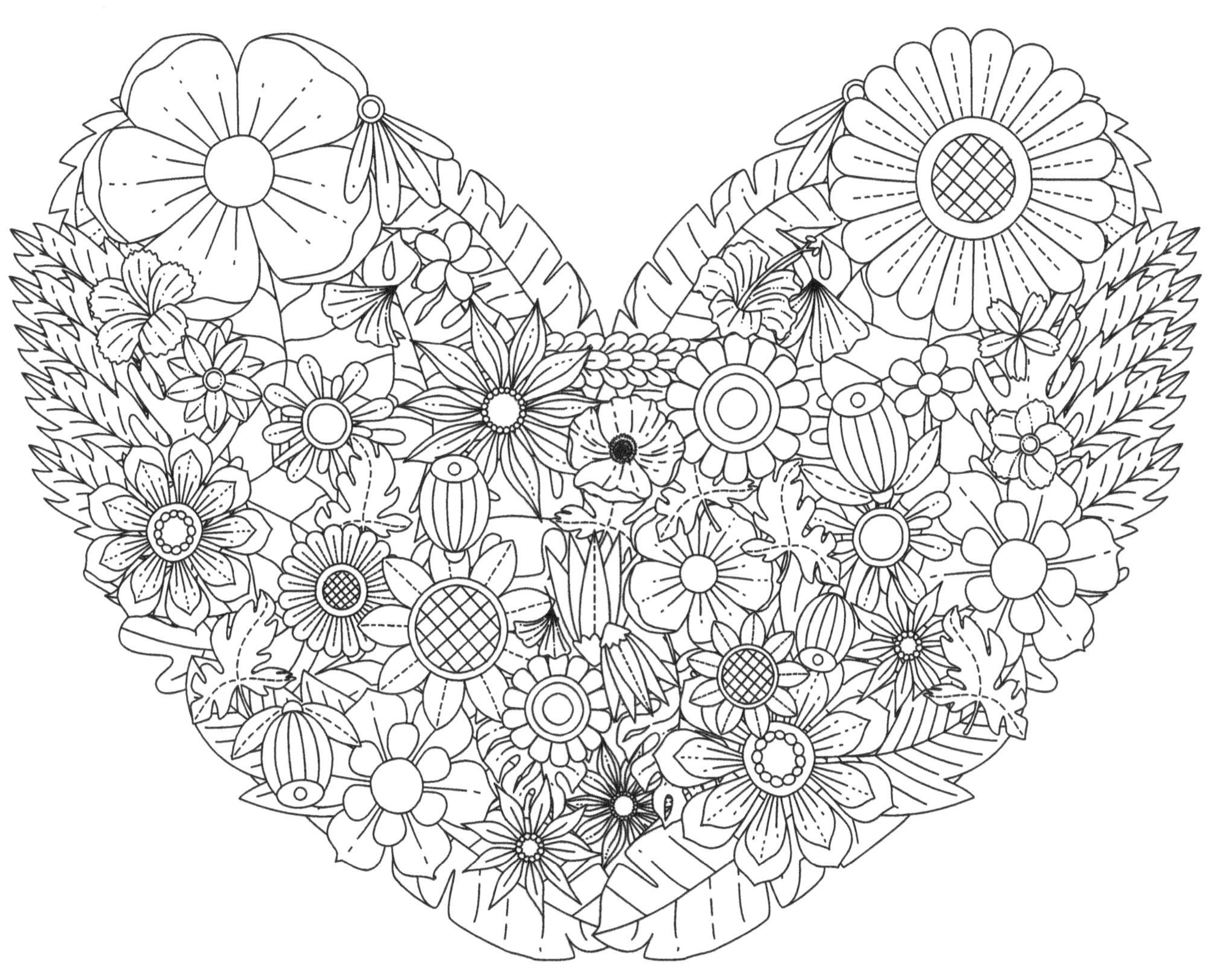

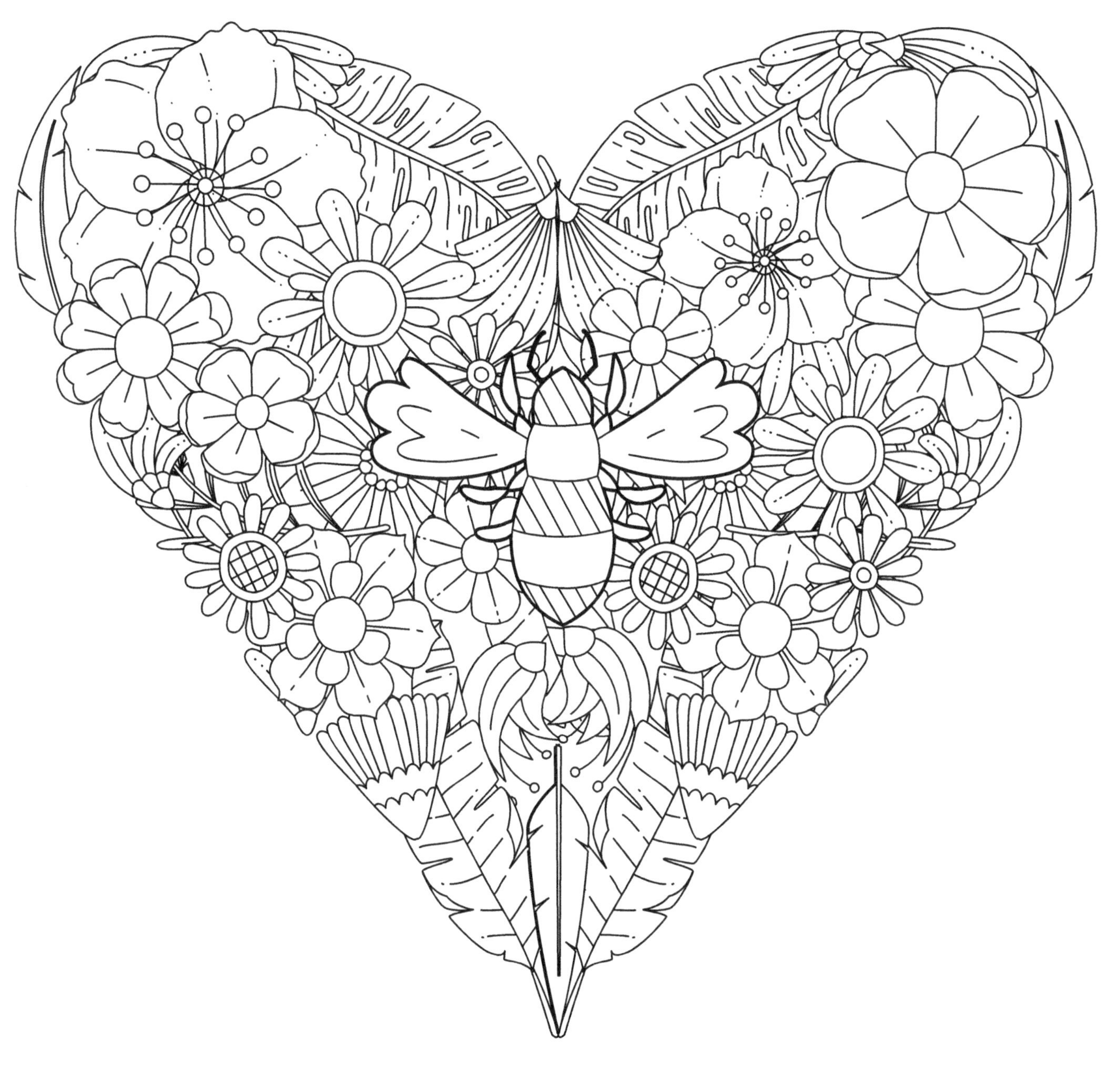

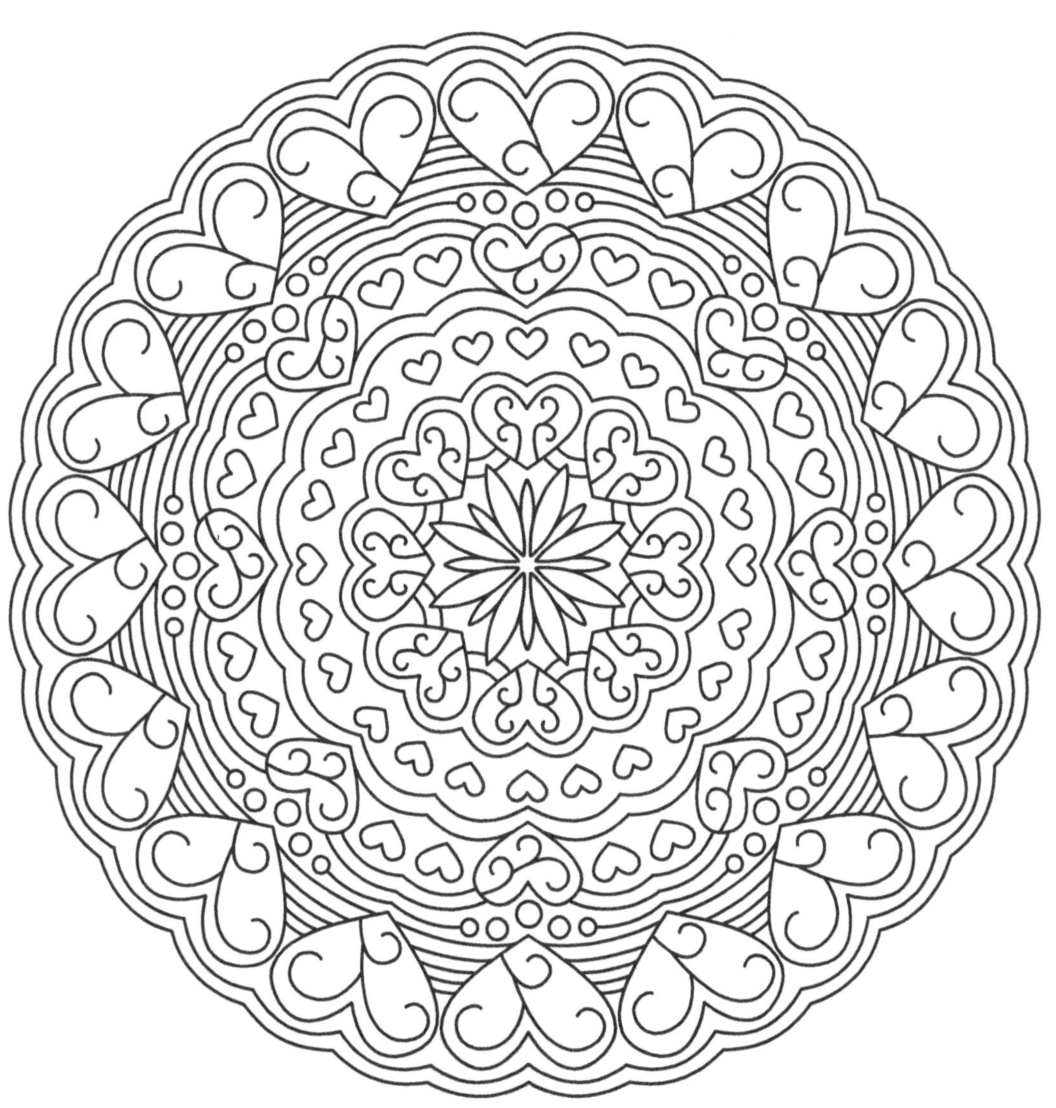

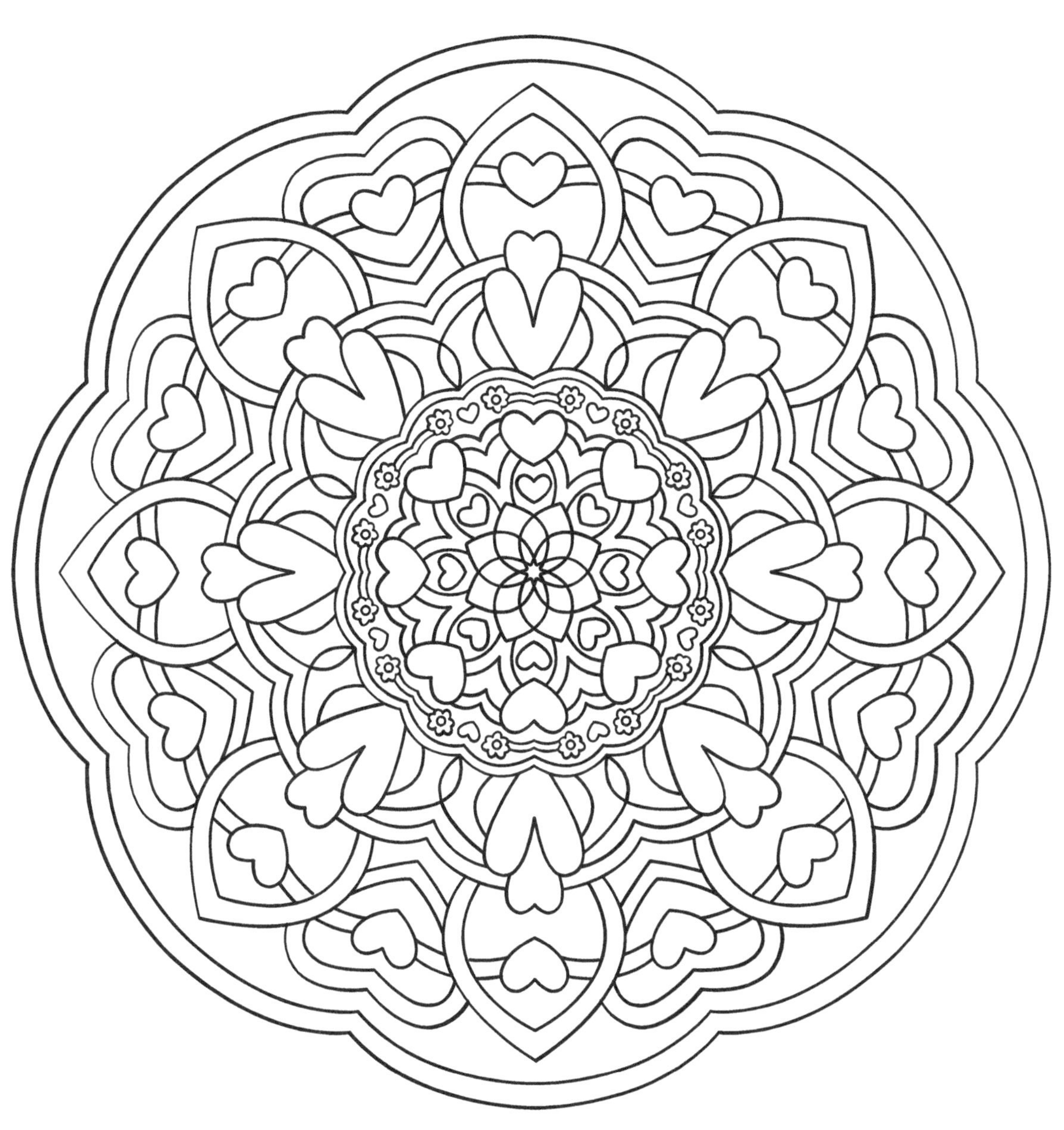

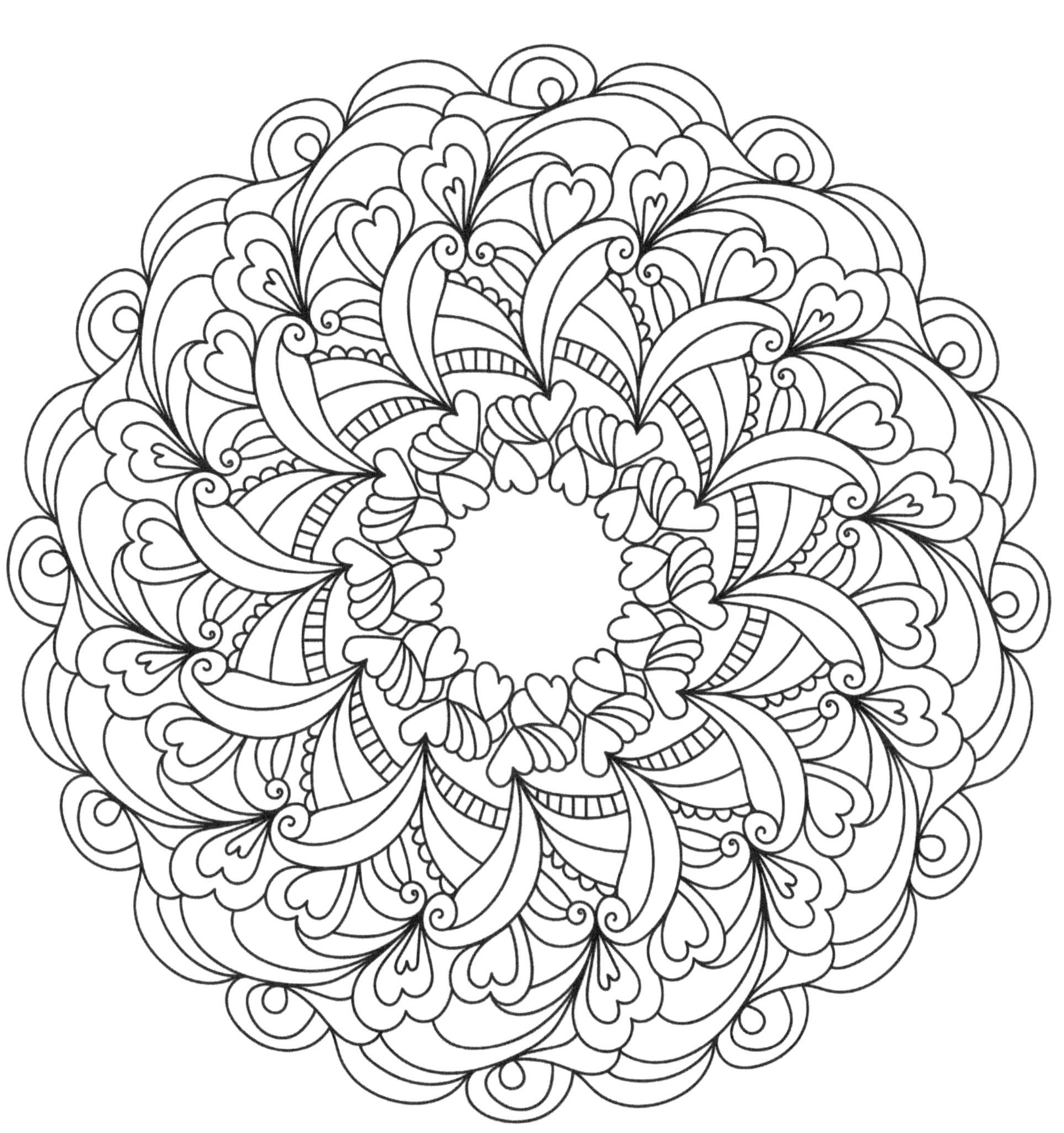

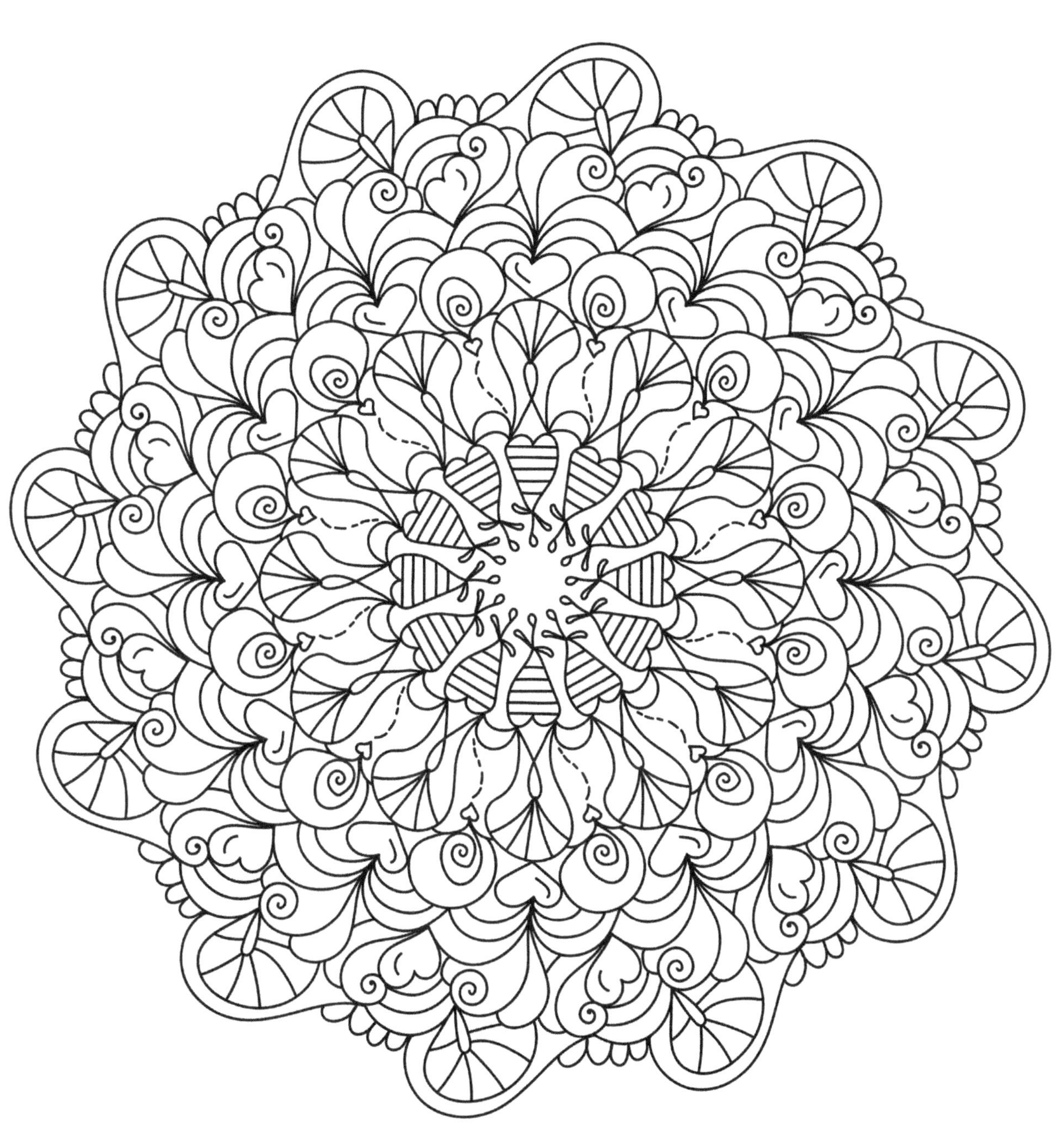

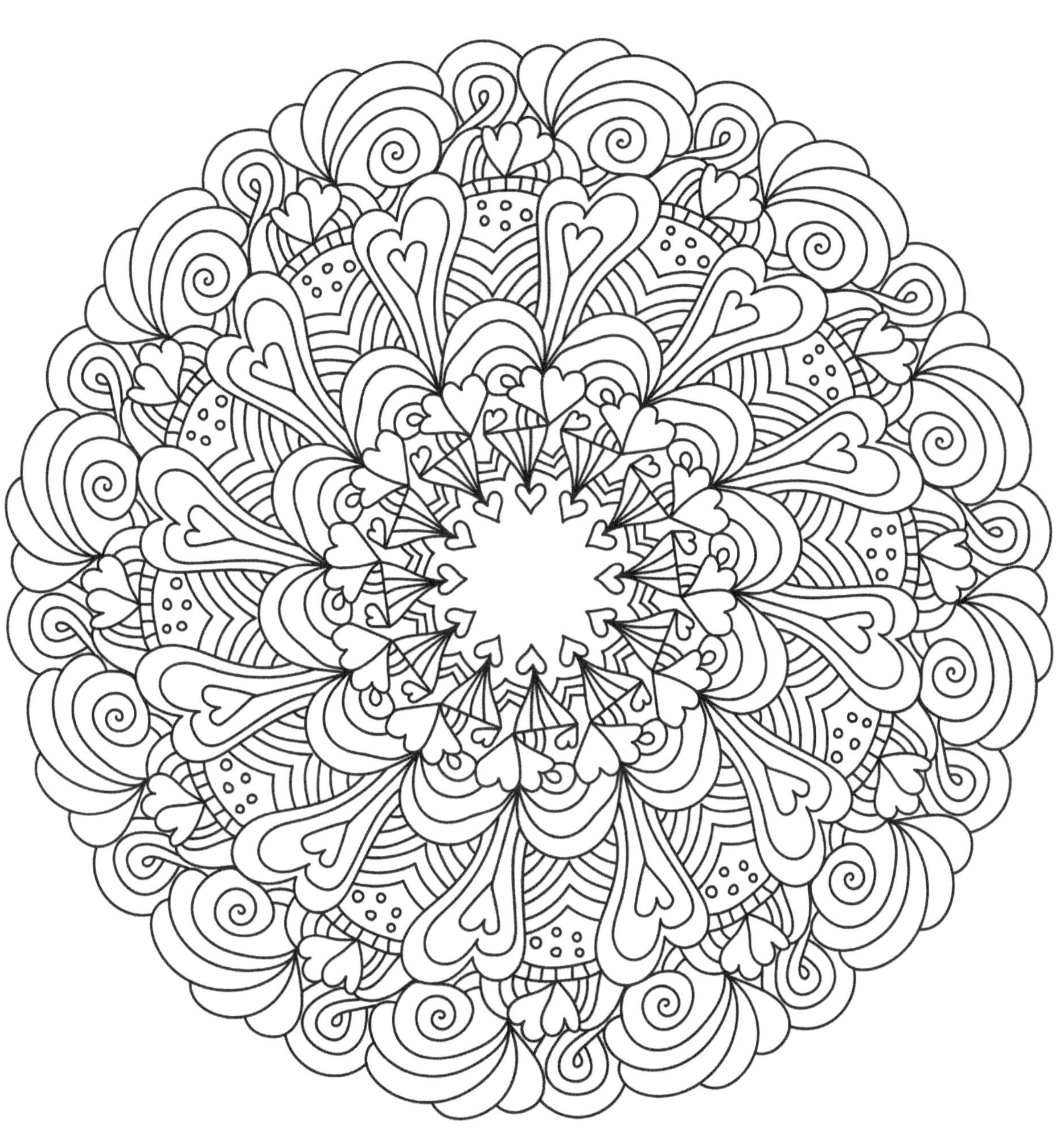

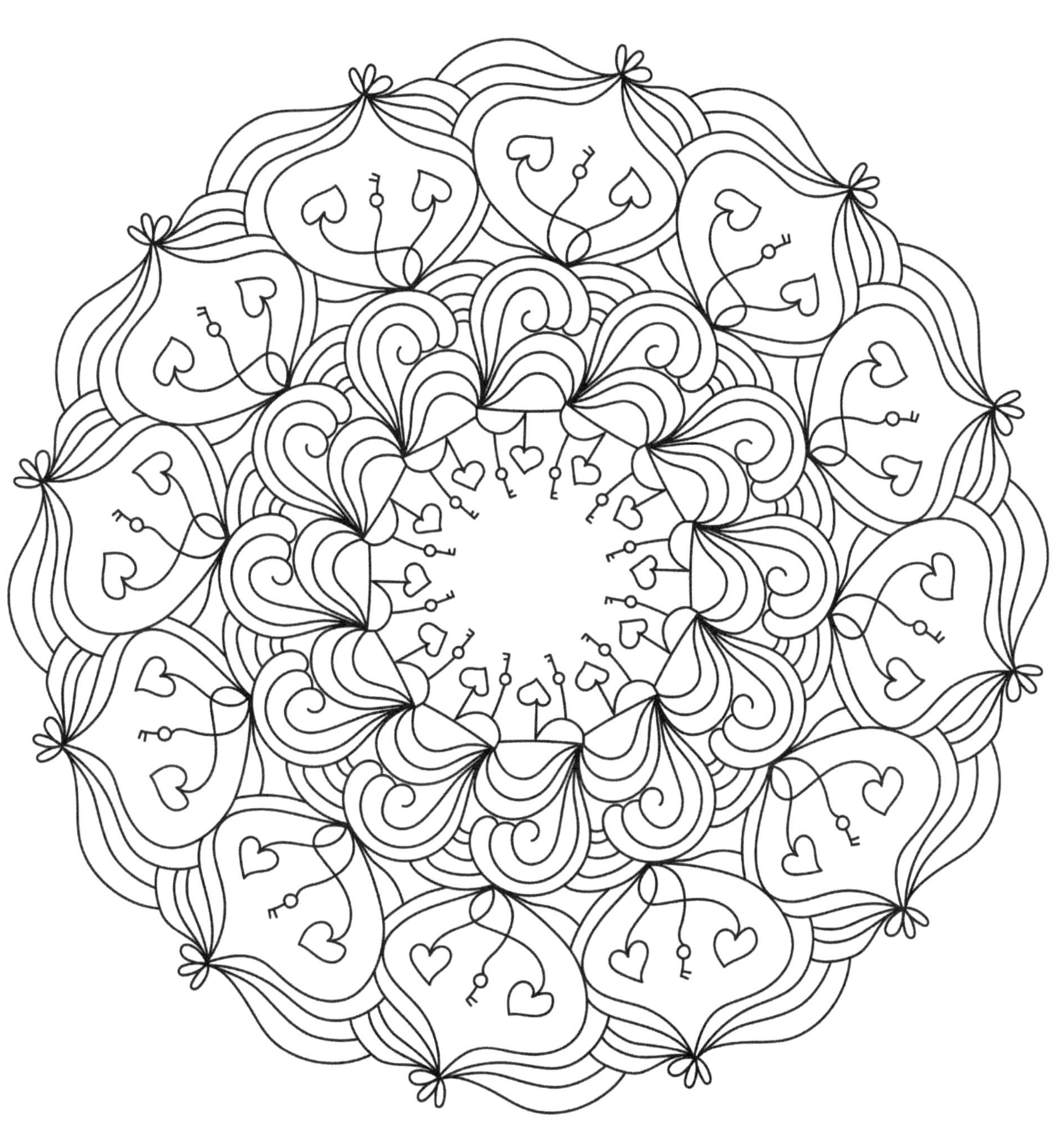

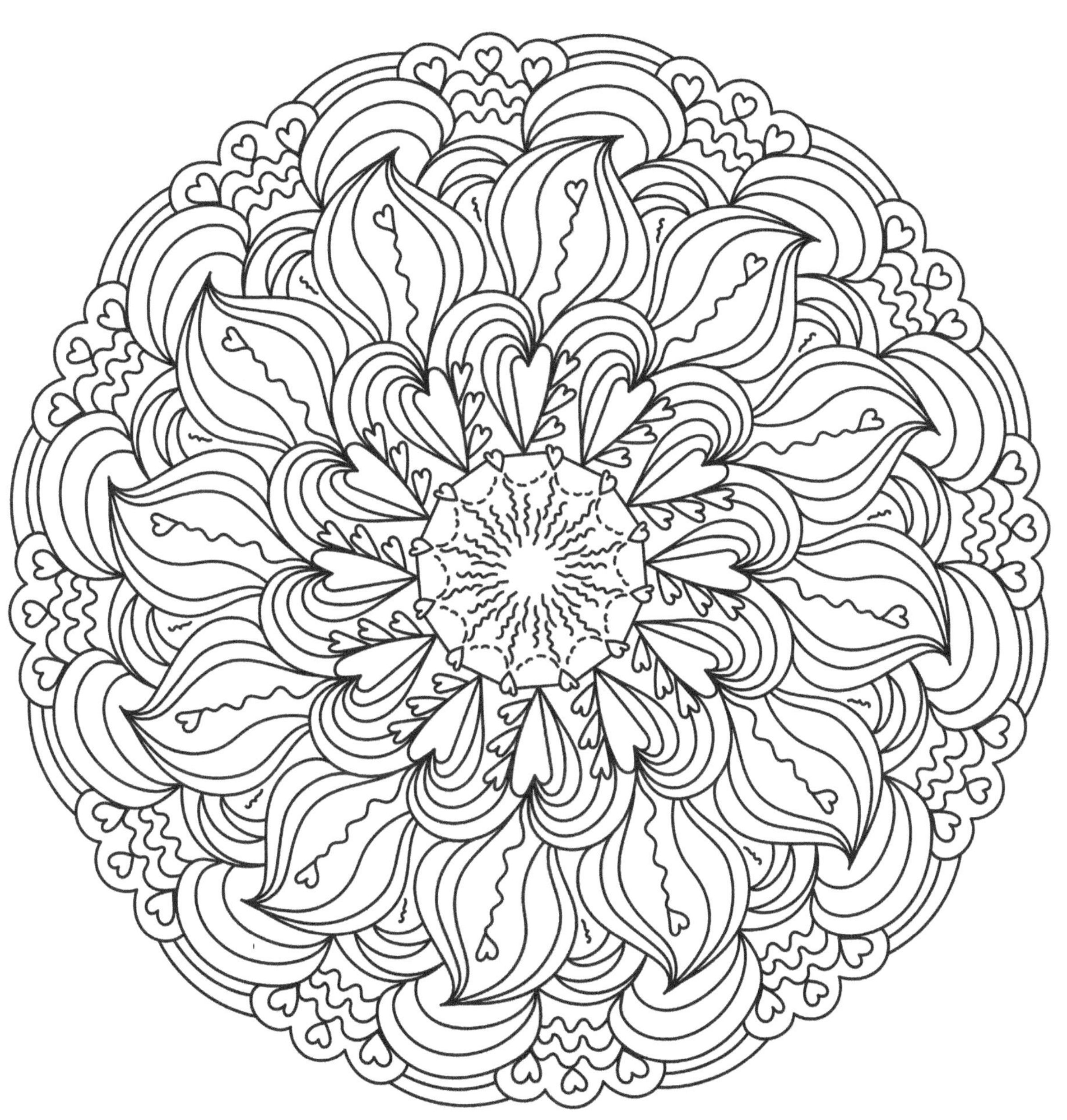

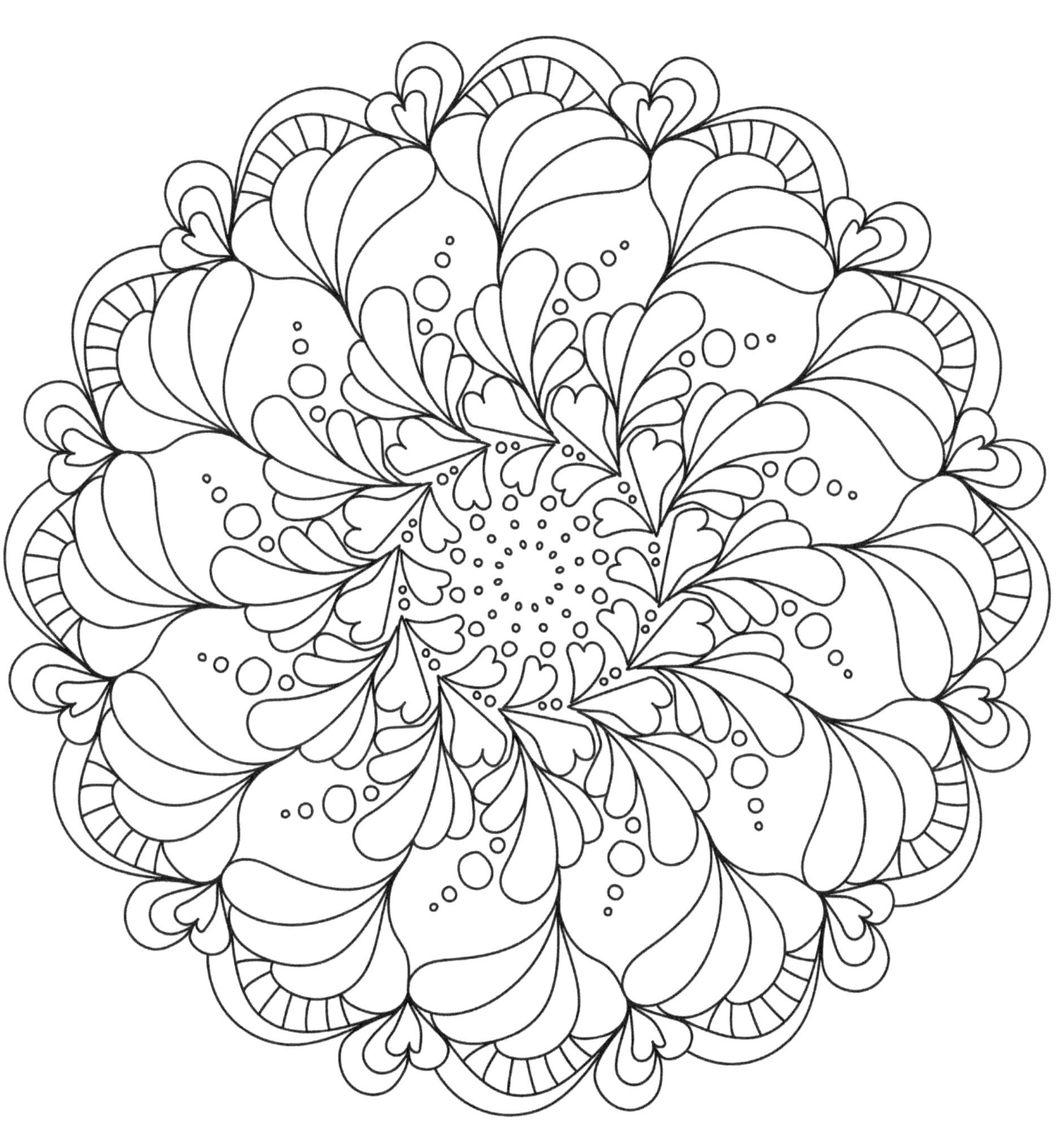

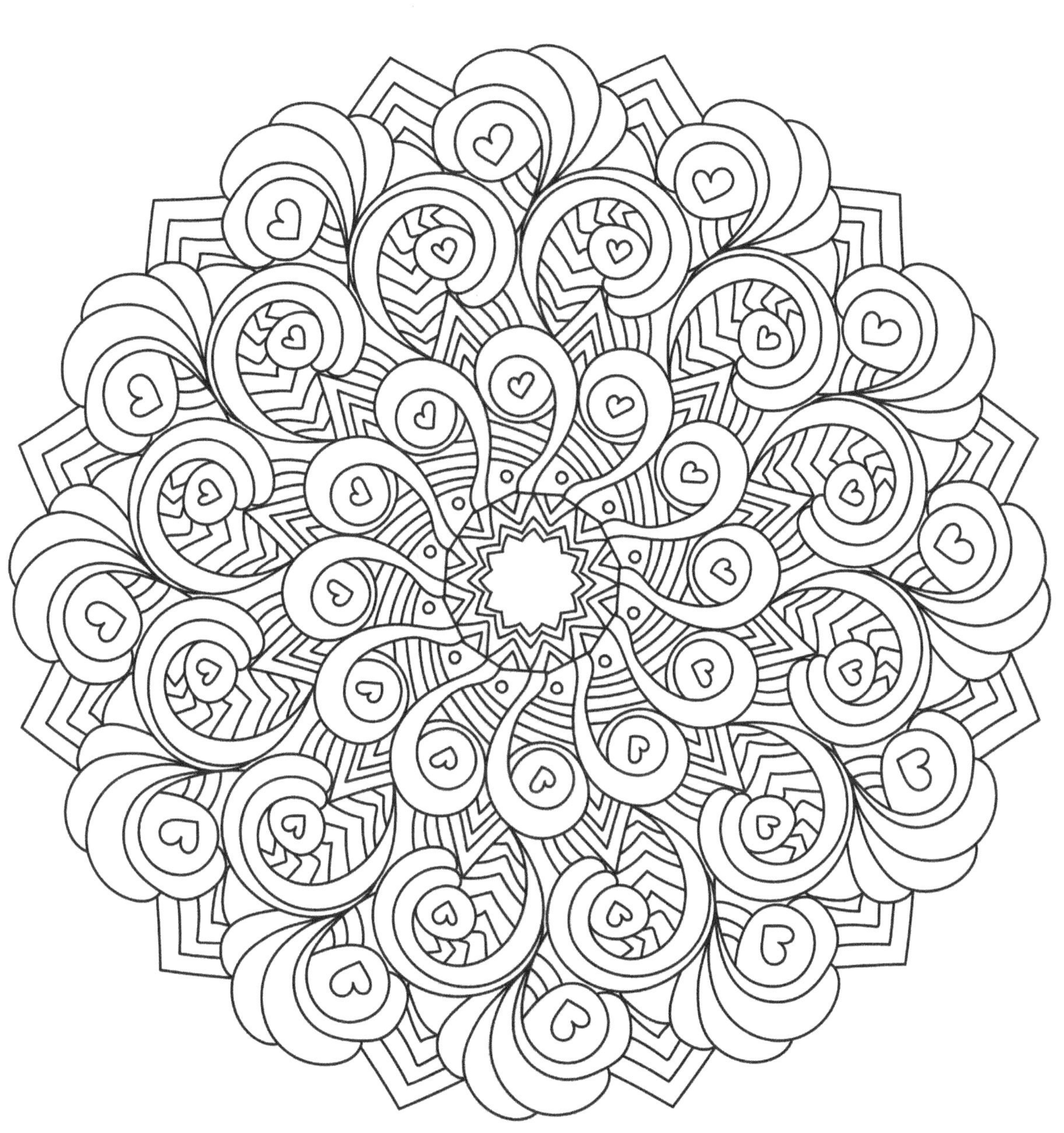

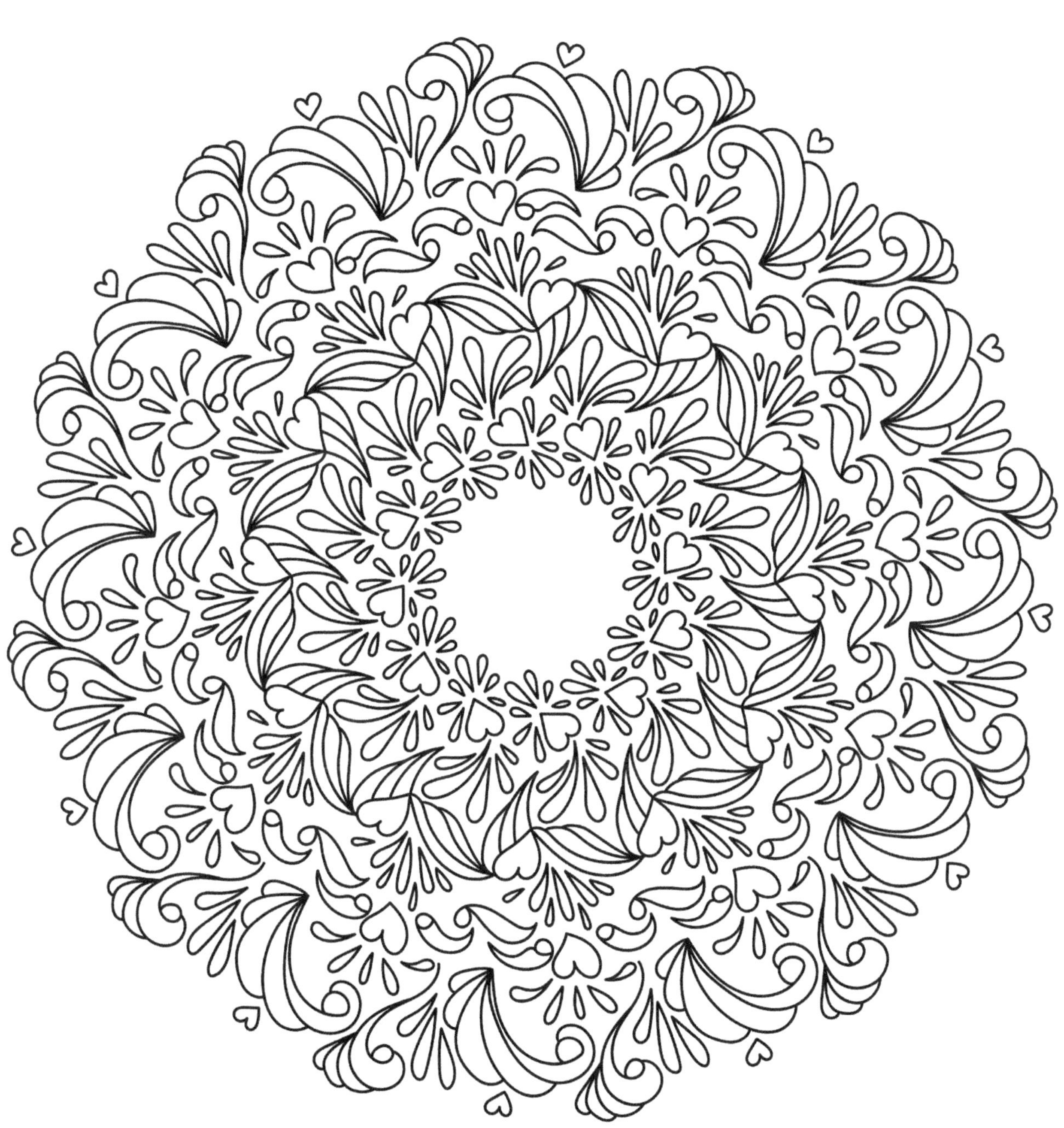

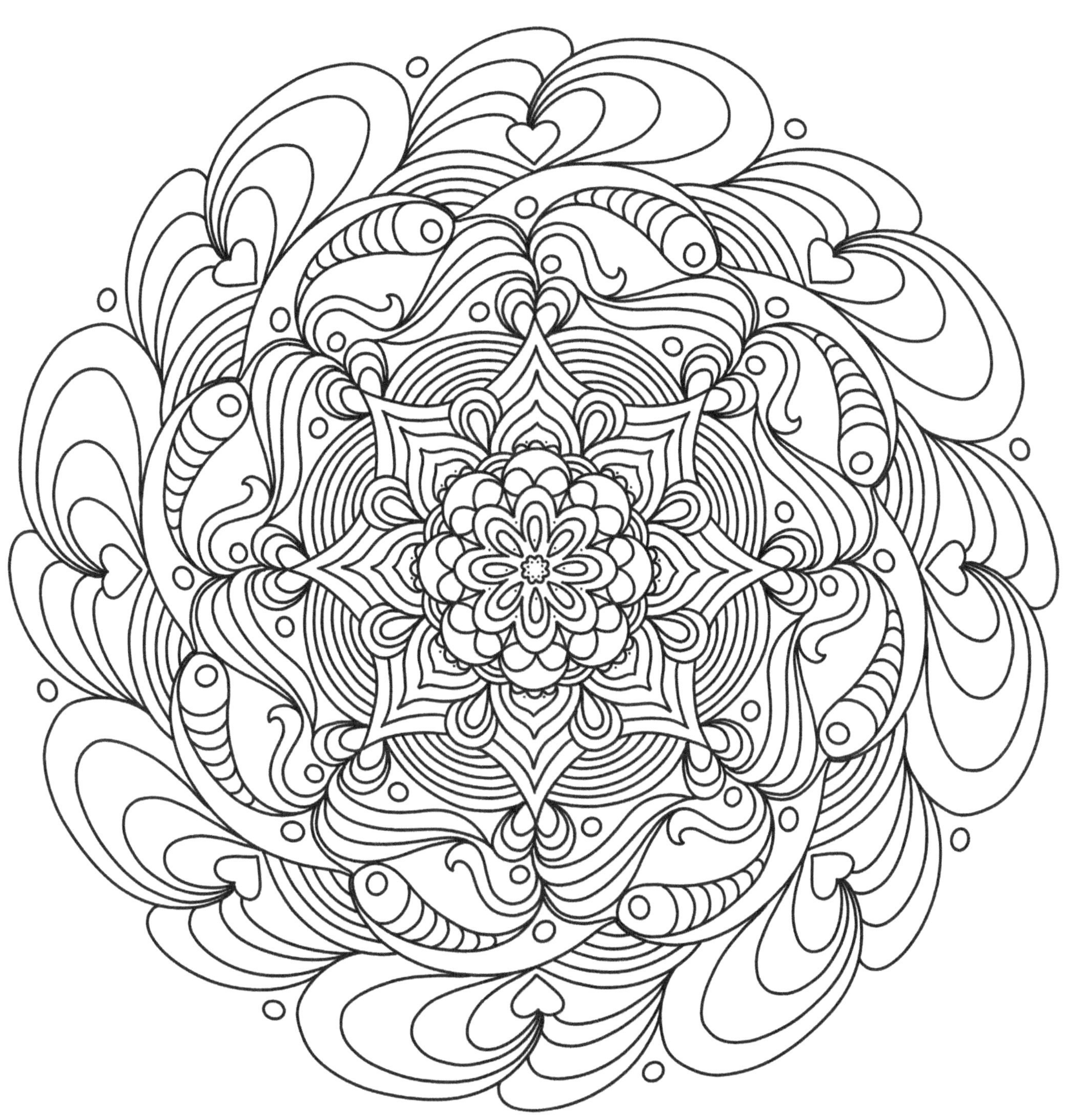

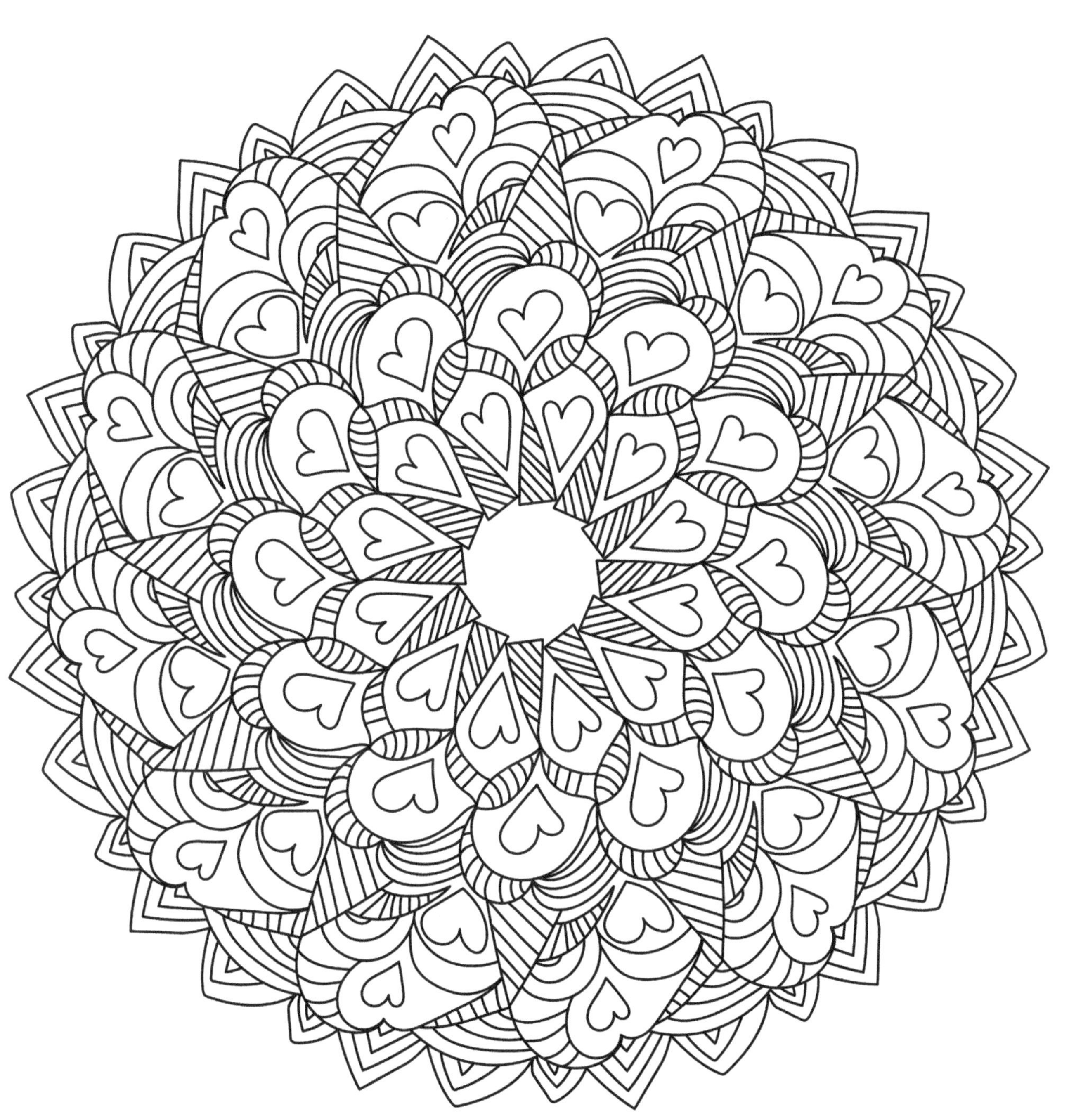

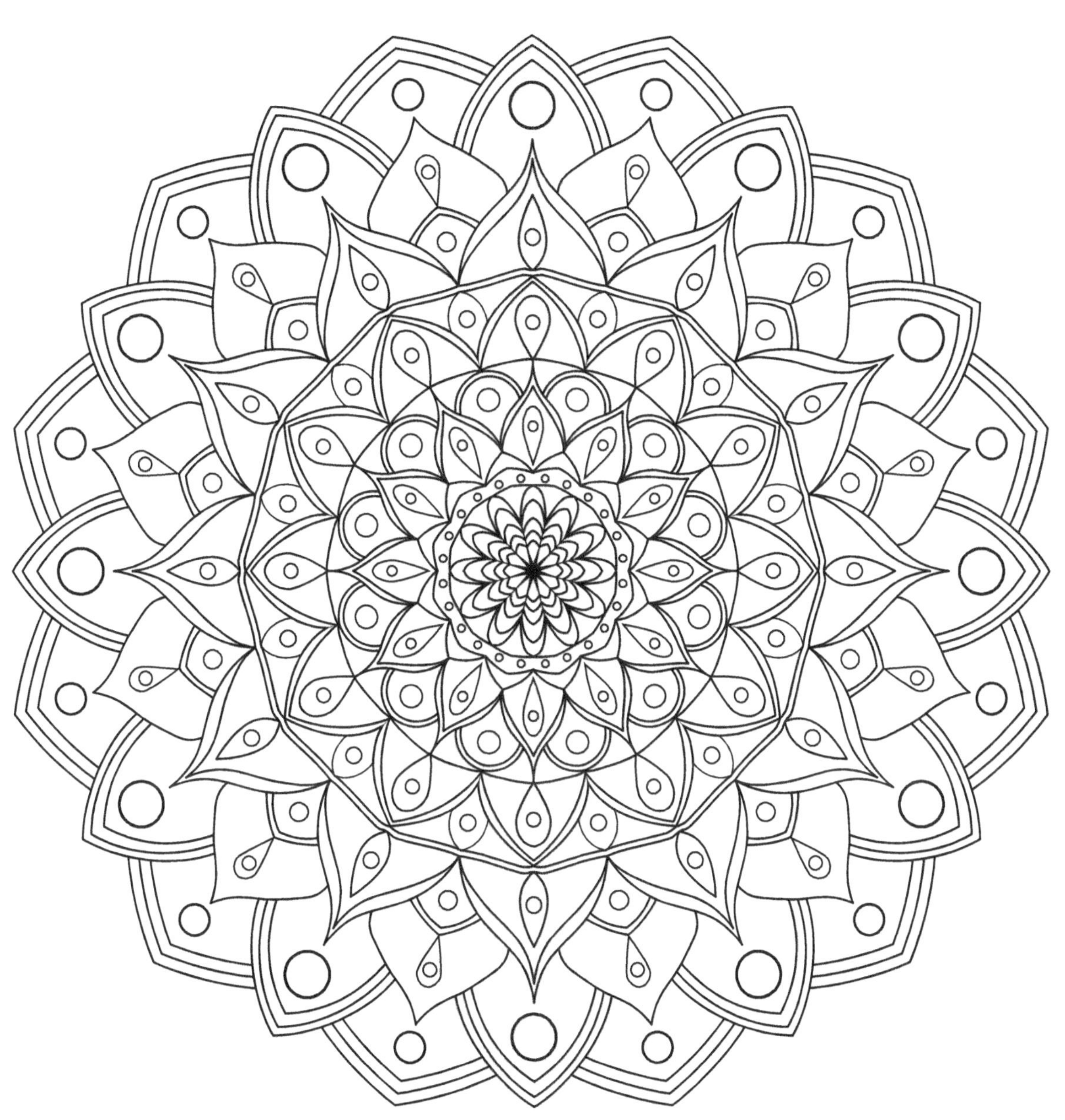

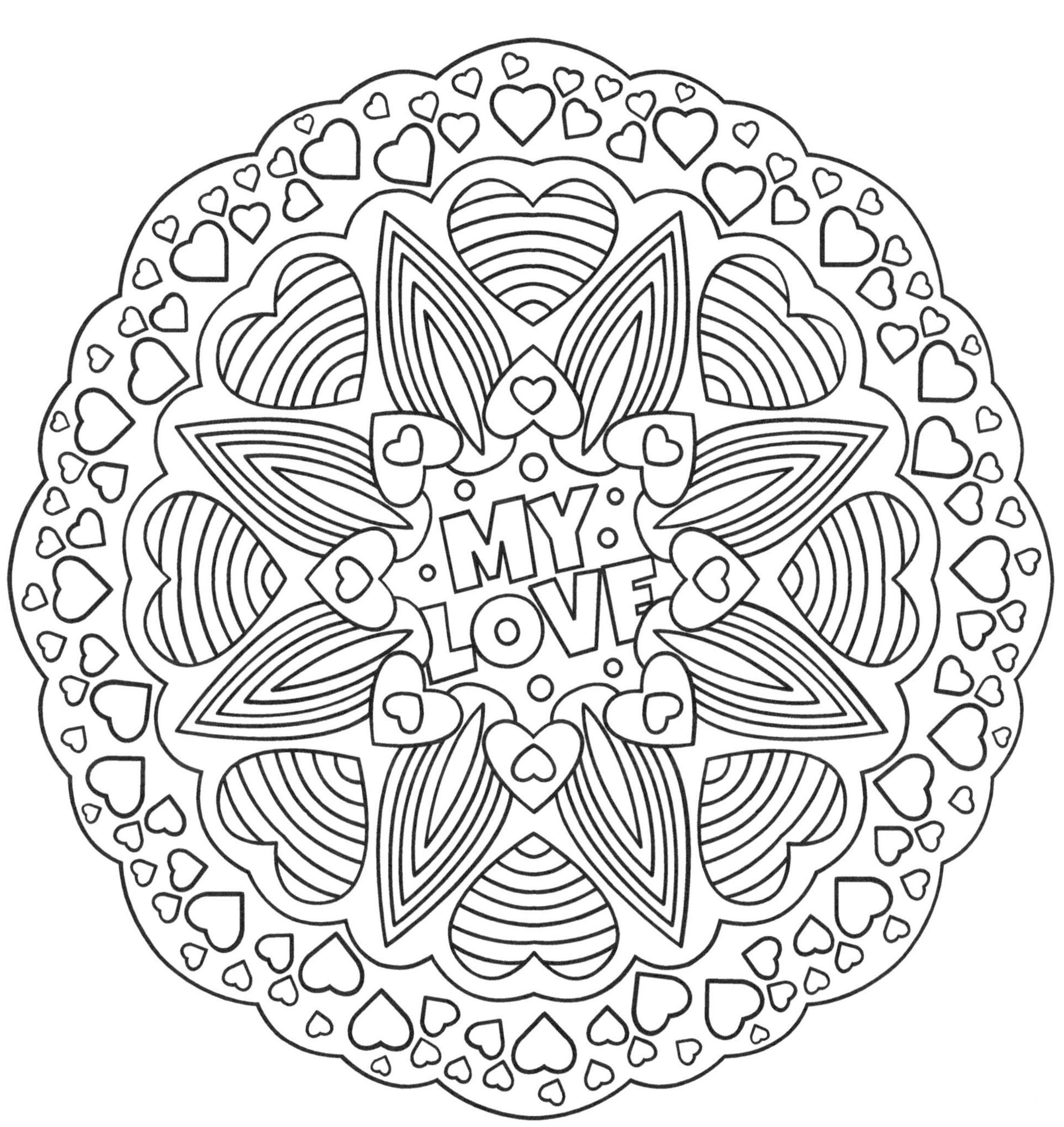

MY
LOVE

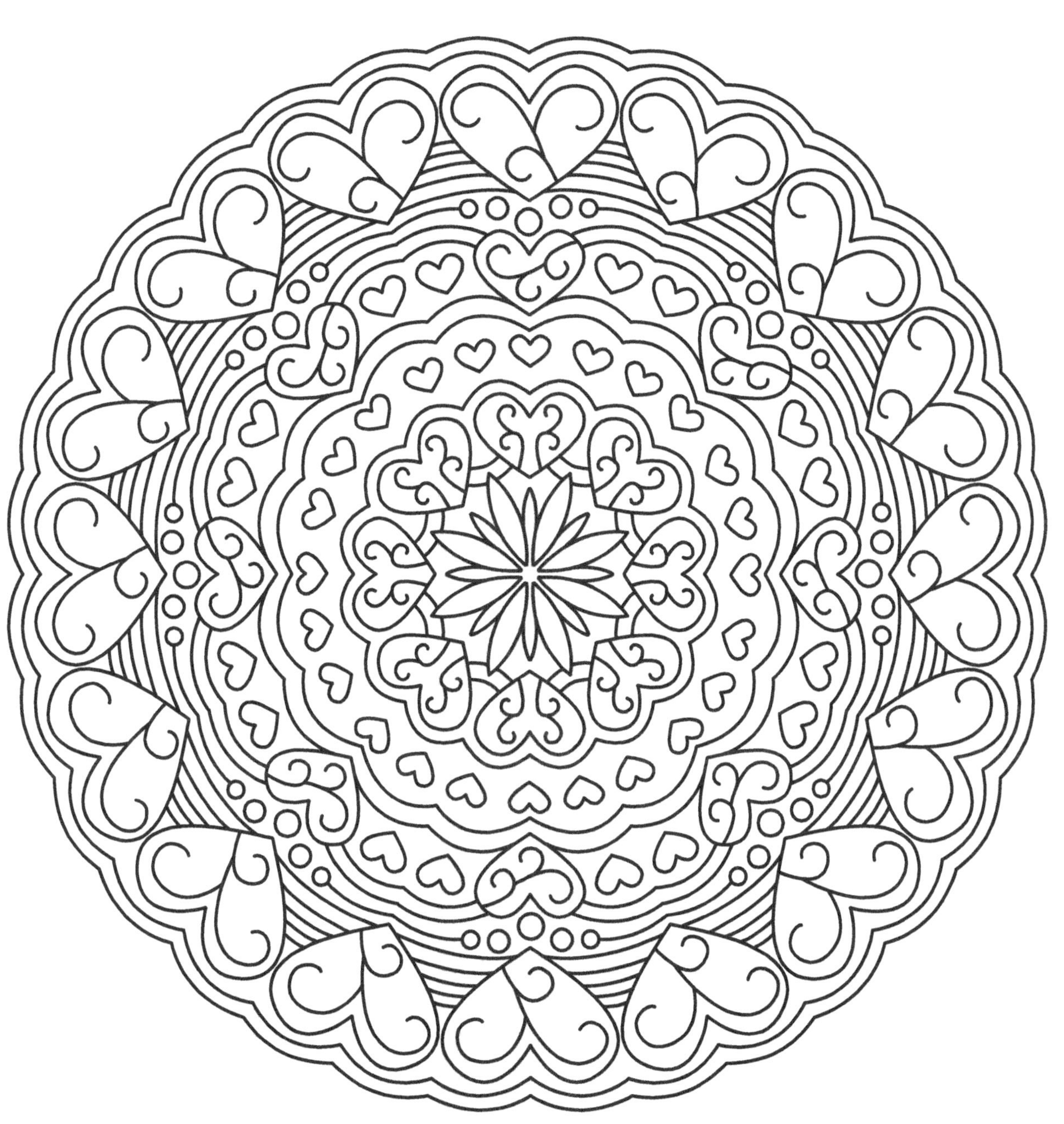

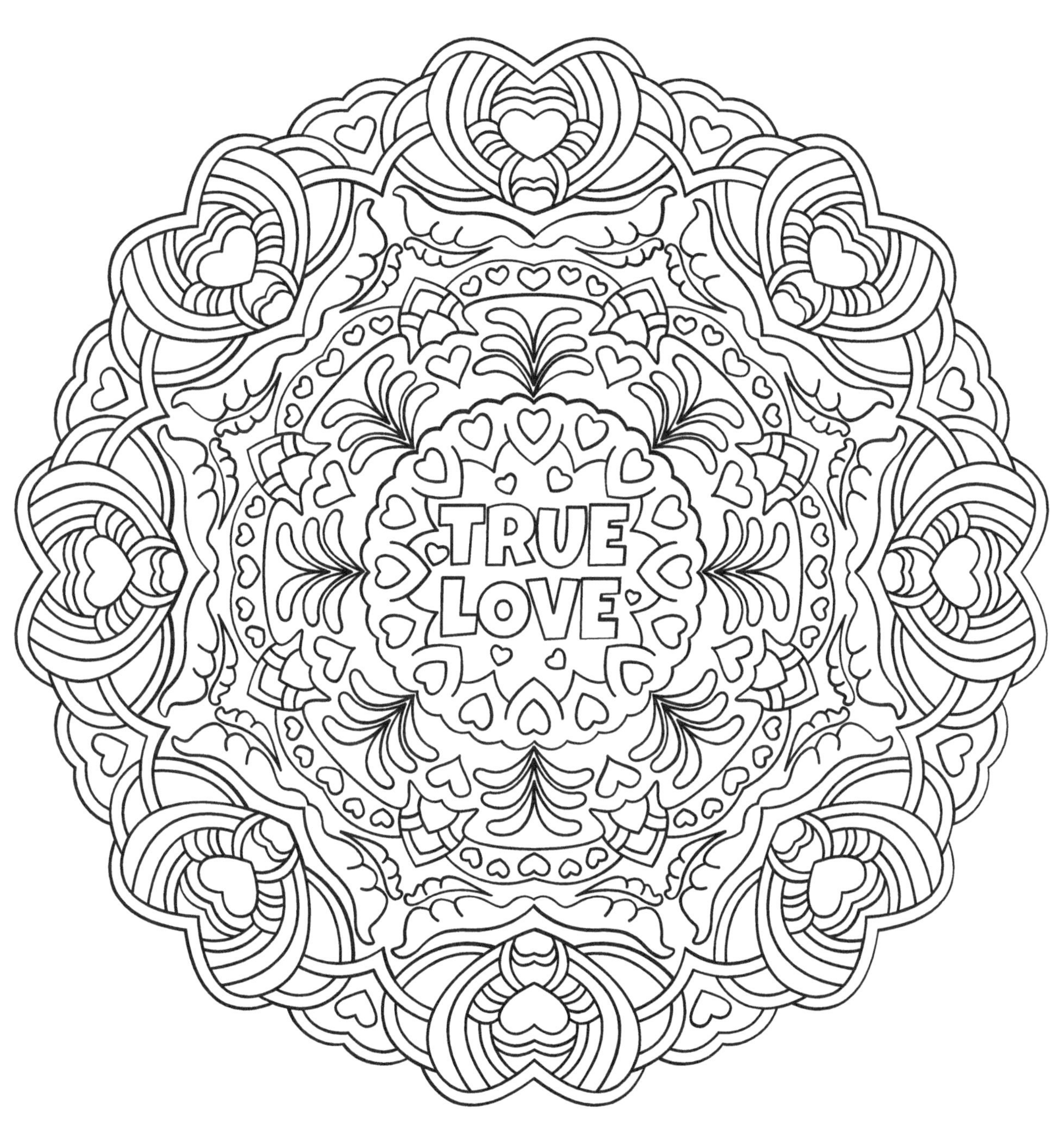
TRUE
LOVE